Diary of a Matelot
1942—1945

Acknowledgement

I should like to thank my
Commanding Officer, Harry Barton,
for kindly writing the Foreword for
this book; and Stuart Eadon for his
encouragement and advice.

Diary of a Matelot 1942—1945

John L. Brown

A Square One Publication

First Published in 1991
by
Square One Publications
Saga House
29/31 Lowesmoor,
Worcester WR1 2RS

©John L. Brown 1991

British Library Cataloguing in Publication Data
Brown, John L
   Diary of a Matelot, 1942—1945
   1. Great Britain, *Royal Navy* 11. World War 2: Naval
   operations
   I. Title
   940.545941

   ISBN 1-872017-40-1

Typeset by Wyvern Typesetting, Worcester.

FOREWORD

John Brown was in the *Formidable* from October 1942 onwards. I joined in April 1944 at Belfast. We were ship mates until he left in October 1945. Forty years later, he telephoned me in Northern Ireland from his home in Manchester.

A play of mine had been broadcast on BBC Radio 4. This play was set in the *Formidable*, 1944/45 and he had heard it and wanted to know whether I was the same Barton. He telephoned me again more recently. He told me of his diary and asked me whether I would read it and suggest what might be done with it. I read it with delight, a marvellous piece of naval and social history. I suggested he offer it to the library of the National Maritime Museum at Greenwich. The Museum accepted it. *Formidable* was a big ship, 23,000 tons, up to eighteen hundred people crammed together in a floating tin box. Each of us saw things the others did not see. For an old shipmate that is the special fascination of the diary. For page after page I might have been reading about some other ship until suddenly there would be an event or person I remembered; and, twice, there were glimpses of myself, a dim forgotten me.

The ship was indeed unhappy around the time of recommissioning at Belfast, when ALTMARK II was found stencilled in large letters on her side. During the refit at Harland and Wolff's, the reduced ship's company became uncomfortable and aimless. The officers and men of the new commission arrived and life suddenly became hard and busy. There was the traditional friction between old and new commissions. Defaulters and absentees multiplied. The Captain solved the problem by getting rid of as many of the old commission as he could. It may be that he exaggerated the difficulties in order to persuade the drafting authorities to replace these people, inventing mutiny, someone said, to achieve his ends. It was an unpleasant time but it passed; and the commission seemed to become excellent as well as memorable. One of its excellent features was Lieutenant John Frewen (the late

Admiral Sir John), a decisive, witty and energetic intellectual much admired by John Brown. He was both Navigating Officer and First Lieutenant. When the ship was at sea he had to spend most of his time on the bridge. He managed nevertheless to be an outstanding Number One; he knew the names of everyone on board, everyone. In 1971, I came across him on holiday in Ethiopia, that strange land. "I am discovering in myself areas of ignorance," he said, "of which I was until now unaware." This younger John Brown was clearly already a thoughtful, compassionate and liberal man. He made friends ashore, enjoying himself wherever the ship took him. Films and theatre meant much to him although he does not mention the pantomime I produced for Christmas 1944, alongside at Gibraltar. (How could he have missed that great production?) He was a Methodist, finding Methodist churches to attend, wherever he was, from Belfast to Australia. He sympathised with the outlook of the Communist Party in the days before the Hitler/Stalin pact. He was a young man who eschewed bigotry and colour-prejudice, in times when such attitudes were more acceptable than they are today. He could take a cool and independent look at officers and establishment generally. He was one of the thousands and thousands of people whose viewpoint gave impetus to the Beveridge Report and the start of the modern health and social services.

I wish he had become an officer. The Navy needed such. In the end he did as well or better. He became a teacher. After his end-of-war leave he went to Shenstone Teacher Training College in Worcester. He taught in primary schools until his retirement in 1970. Lucky children to have had a teacher of such quality and such warmth.

Harry Barton 1989
(Captain A.H. Barton C.B.E., R.N. (retd.)

1942

On June 16th 1942 I had to report to *HMS Royal Arthur*. Naturally I had very mixed feelings on the matter, an awareness of the horrors of war, perhaps its futility although necessary because there seemed no alternative, and yet a pleasant anticipation of new surroundings, new experiences and new friends (not that I had not been blessed with good companions) and sharing the outlook of other people and thus a broadening of my mind.

On arriving at Skegness I, and a few more raw recruits, were met at the station by a short, elderly CPO who informed us that the boat would draw alongside soon to take us to the ship. Spirits were high, and higher still when our boat arrived, it was a small enclosed lorry, which carried us to the *Royal Arthur* through the pleasant seaside resort of Skegness. It seemed somewhat incongruous to be taken for training whilst holiday makers were strolling the wide streets.

On nearing the *Royal Arthur* we passed many of the not so raw recruits marching back to the ship. They were dressed in white shorts, green, red or blue football shirts and a naval cap, some matelot some fore and aft. Our arrival was greeted by jeers, such as "Get a number": "You'll soon learn": "Why don't you join up?" Our replies were wasted, being equally unintelligent.

The *Royal Arthur* was previously Butlin's Holiday Camp, a huge but compact campus. Six large halls extended along the front of the ship—the Theatre, and Windsor, Kent, York, Gloucester and Empress Halls. On the centre hall was still discernable the Butlin Motto—OUR TRUE INTENT IS ALL FOR YOUR DELIGHT. Needless to say this caption had a humourous twist applied to it when you were once inboard.

The ship was well equipped; two swimming pools with

7

high and low diving boards, a Cinema, Theatre, Gymnasium, Tennis Courts, Playing Fields, Canals, etc.

Long rows of well constructed chalets lay behind the halls, and each was divided by a strip of lawn edged by a narrow flower bed. Further behind lay the sand dunes.

On reporting our arrival we were placed in the chalets reserved for the Incoming Draft. My companion for the night was Arthur Barnes of Stoke. After tea we took stock of the ship and gave it full marks.

The next few days were spent in being kitted up; a continual round of falling in and journeying round the ship and acquiring en route hammock, respirator, kit, etc. Interspersed with this formality were lectures from the Commander, Chaplain and MO.

As I was non-conformist I attended with the very few, typed as Sheffield Wednesdays,the Rev. Piggott's chalet. He was young, breezy and full of good common sense, someone to whom you took immediately.

I was placed in the Accountancy Branch as a Supply Assistant, much to my chagrin. The uniform was a cross between that of a taxi driver and a Workhouse inmate. Despite the advice from the PO in charge of our class I made two requests to transfer to some other branch, Stoker, Wireless Tel. etc. The requests were refused.

A class of 37 SA's having been formed a block of chalets was allotted to us, my chalet mates this time were Jock Aitken of Cowburn and Charlie Bevan of London. Later on, after Jock's being drafted another Scot, Jock Geary, was placed in our chalet.

We learned that our stay at the R.A. was for five weeks' disciplinary training after which we would be drafted to the Naval School of Accountancy in London.

Disciplinary training consisted of square bashing, rifle drill, bayonet practice, a rudimentary knowledge of seamanship, pulling in the cutter and whaler, a few knots and Duty Class.

Duty Class had to perform all the menial tasks of the ship—helping in the galley; sweeping up what appeared

8

milions of square miles of roads; skirmishing among the flower beds for fag-ends, nutty paper etc.; cleaning the Heads (toilets to you) and did I not get my share and everybody else's share of this task?; sand bag filling and road block construction etc. Looking back we got a great deal of fun out of it.

Among the jobs of Duty Class was helping the gardener, a job which I coveted and won by judicious flanneling. A few well directed remarks about lobelia, alyssum, wall flowers and forget-me-nots would make a colourful display won for me a scrounging job.

Meals were taken in the large halls.The classes fell in and marched at a given signal. Everything was orderly until the entrance of the hall was reached when pandemonium broke out in a wild scramble for a seat. A number of us found means of stopping this practice and that of lifting the biggest share of food. Four members of each class took duties in turn as cooks for the class. This did not mean actually cooking, but obtaining it from the galley, setting the table, and washing the crockery and cutlery afterwards.

Square bashing was a different matter. On the whole I thoroughly enjoyed it but always overhead was the sword of Damocles, Dusty Miller, a small disgruntled PO. He took exception to all ratings in fore and aft rig. He boasted that he was the only sane person in the ship and a ticket to prove it. Was it a discharge from some asylum? At the end of the course, I think I understood that he was doing it for our own good and for our self preservation. We got him for the whole of the day and every day and from the word go we thought he must be mad. He bullied, kicked, hit, punched, swore and insulted us the whole of the time we had him. I think he managed to get us to successfully perform perfectly synchronised movements. After the heat of the day, the hardness of the roads, Dusty's high speed Left-Right, the hardness of our beds was luxury indeed. Four members of the class who had come in for physical abuse complained, but there was no redress. Weeks later on the completion of the course, when we were talking to him,

9

he gave us invaluable hints on surviving, on how to dhobi your clothes, and then I knew he was really on our side, and I thanked him.

The first duty after breakfast was Divisions, which we came to know as Bennett's Circus, after the Ship's Commander. Each class doubled round the halls for ten minutes to the strains of the Royal Marine Band, and the constant prodding from PO's, CPO's, Officers, and anyone who assumed authority, to change step, elbows up, keep in line, knees up, and a dozen more of oft repeated and often contradictory commands. After the circus we assembled for the hoisting of the colours on the Quarter Deck, Prayers, the National Anthem, after which we followed the day's routine. Sunday morning was always impressive. This was the day when we marched past the Commander, or some other important personage. We were always assembled for what appeared hours before the show started at the side of the Empress Hall, a place which became known as the marshalling yard. Here we had a good view of the various branches and the colourful uniforms of the foreign seamen, Norwegians, Belgians, French and Greeks. The cool bright colour of the Norwegian blue jean collar, their jaunty cap, and their uninterrupted left or right turn, quick march never failed to win our admiration Each contingent marched with their colours at their head.

The march past was always witnessed by small crowds of holiday makers from Skegness who lined the road which passed the camp on the elevated roadway. When passing the person taking the salute the order "Eyes right" was given. No doubt it was an impressive show, arms were swung at shoulder height with the thumb bent upwards to give the appearance of greater height of the arm, whilst heads jerked simultaneously to the right on passing the stand.

The march past being over the Roman Catholics and Non-conformists fell out to attend Services in their respective halls set aside for that purpose. About a thousand ratings attended the Non-conformist Hall, our entrance being accompanied by Handel's *Largo*, the Recessional was always *The Holy City*. The first hymn was without fail *Eternal Father Strong to Save*. A lesson was read by an officer, a solo would be given invariably by a rating, but the outstanding feature of the Service was the riveting and eloquent address of ten minutes by the Rev. Piggott and his moving prayers. After service communion was held in the Scouts' Hut for those who wished to receive it. The service was conducted by the chaplain assisted by ratings.

I should mention that the music at the service was provided by a unique combination of piano, accordions, saxophones and whatever instrument you brought along. Nevertheless the atmosphere was most reverent.

A Fellowship Meeting was held on Thursday evenings in the little church. This was conducted by the ratings themselves either in the form of a prayer meeting, or an address by one of the ratings. There were many really good local preachers amongst the lads. The Rev. Piggott always showed at the end and gave the benediction.

A few days after my arrival Ken Taylor, a local friend, was placed in the chalet next to mine, and until that moment I had failed to find him among all the recruits. Luckily he was in the same watch as me and consequently our shore leaves were spent together. Ken was being trained as a bunting tosser, his course lasting six months.

Liberty leave was on alternative days from 4.15pm and 1.30pm on Saturdays and Sundays until 22.00. Hundreds fell in for inspection and marched to the gates where buses awaited to take us to Skegness. There was little to do here except get a meal at the NAAFI or YMCA or at Service Clubs, or queue up for the Cinema. I usually went to Roman Bank or Ingoldmells Methodist Clubs where billiards, table tennis and refreshments at reasonable prices could be had. Dancing at Skegness was not too good. A few hotels held dances but the rooms were really small whilst the Sun Castle Ballroom, although good, was not much bigger than the hotels.

The whole of my stay at RA was one of unbroken hot

weather, and as all of our life was spent out of doors at Drill, PT or Recreational Training on the Sports Fields I benefited considerably. I should have mentioned Ingoldmells and its ancient church and exceptionally good WVS canteen.

A mention of the RA would not be complete without its anthem, a baudy jingle sung with great gusto as is the invariable custom when matelots gather together. Here are some of the lines:-

Why don't you join up, why don't you join up, why
don't you join old Butlins Navy?
Ten bob a week, fuck all to eat, marching round the
Quarter Deck with blisters on your feet
Why don't you join up, why don't you join up, why
don't you join old Butlin's Navy?
I wouldn't give a tanner for the whole darn lot, Sailors,
I've shit 'em.

It was the custom of classes on draft to stand on their chairs at their last tea time and sing *Auld Lang Syne*, a custom which died hard despite the turbulent scenes and raucous comments of those being left behind. Sometimes attempts were made to stop this singing by the duty officer, in which case the scoffers who attempted to break up the choir then joined them and sang vigorously.

We followed the custom when we were ready to leave then we packed our kit, took it to the luggage room, and attended to the many jobs attendant on one's departure. We arose very early the next morning, having slept without blanket, and swallowed an unappetising breakfast in an atmosphere of gloom through which passed stealthy figures tired after a night's watch. We had ridiculed the RA, cursed it, its food and routine, and now on the point of departure it dawned upon us that here, we had enjoyed comradeship.

The hoarse barking of the PO caused us to assemble; articles were still being packed or stuffed or coaxed into our attache cases or pockets and in this ordered confusion we took our places on the buses lined up to take us to

Skegness. A further sorting out took place and we climbed thankfully into the reserved railway compartments.

The weary journey through a monotonous countryside was whiled away with whist, solo, nap, etc. On nearing London the stations were crowding with people on their way to business. Whether it was our uniforms, our sleepless looks, or whatever, I don't know but newspapers were showered on us by the passengers.

At Kings Cross Station the usual bustle of men on draft attracted many bystanders. Hammocks securely lashed, kit bags bulging until they looked as if to burst open at any moment, and our attendant paraphernalia, were thrown on trucks as we hurried to the awaiting lorries, sorry ships. Meanwhile we had a meal at the Salvation Army Caledonian Canteen adjoining the station after which we were driven, or should it be sailed, to HMS *President V* at Highgate, North London.

I suppose northerners are a little suspicious about Londoners, their supposed lack of hospitality, totally unfounded, and the ship appeared most inviting.

We assembled on the Quarter Deck, no, it was the quadrangle, for the *President V* was previously Highgate Grammar School, and soon we were welcomed by the Skipper, Captain Woodhouse. I use the word "welcome" because it was a gracious welcome, with hopes for happy remembrances of our new ship and comfort while we were there, and promises to do everything to make our stay and our training as comfortable as possible. This was the Navy 1942.

We were soon fixed up in our sleeping quarters. These were previously the chemistry laboratories of the school, but now two-tiered beds lined the bulkheads. After tea Norman Lewis of Sunderland, Arthur Barrow and I strolled over Hampstead Heath nearby, and revelled in the prospects of ten happy weeks to come. The following morning we were addressed by the Skipper at great length; he stressed the importance of our duties and the necessity of working hard. The speech also informed us of the abounding facilities the *President V* provided, its opportunities for social intercourse, the high esteem in which the ratings of the ship was held by the people of Highgate, and the absence of compulsion to work if we were so inclined.

Captain Woodhouse outlined his ideas, the placing of men on their honour and the good results which had been obtained that way.Frequently occur ring in his speech was the remark: "I love you men", so much so that we nicknamed him "The Great Lover."

Routine of the ship was simple. We assembled in the great hall at 8.40 and greeted the Skipper's entrance with the low murmer of "Good morning, Sir." This was St. Michael's of Will Hay's sketch come to life. Meanwhile the colours had been hoisted, the ceremony being preceded by the wavering and frequently shrill notes of the bugler, whilst the Duty Class presented arms. Following this we doubled across the small yard to the Quarter Deck, the School's Hall.

The Quarter Deck possessed a very good floor and an excellent stage. The walls were panelled in oak upon which had been inscribed the school's scholarship successes, which were truly a remarkable and exceptional record.

We were marshalled in our respective classes and inspected, stood to attention, stood at ease, meanwhile stepping forward and backward one pace until all the classes had been reported to the Skipper by the Divisional Officers.

Morning prayers followed and then a hymn was sung. The Skipper invariably chose *For ever with the Lord* as the hymn to be sung. On dismissal we marched in formation across the yard whilst he looked down upon us from a balcony.

The course consisted of lectures in Naval Stores, Victualling, Clothing, Mess Traps, Typing and Recreational Training. A general session was generally included once a week. There were two lectures each morning divided by a stand-easy from 10.45 — 11.05. Morning lectures finished at 12.30. Afternoon work commenced at 14.30 and finished at

16.15, a ten minutes stand-easy being enjoyed. Each class acted as duty class for one week during which lectures for them were suspended.

I was fortunate in that my first week was spent in getting acquainted with the ship and my second week was in duty class. During this time I slept on the ship, with interruptions from air raids, during which we were a fire fighting party.

Afternoon leave was granted to each watch on alternative afternoons and on these occasions we toured London. The remainder of the time was spent in scrubbing and sweeping decks, painting bulkheads, sentry and fire-watching, and generally keeping the place clean. If on guard at the entrance we kept a look-out and saluted funerals.

President V possessed an open air swimming pool and good sports grounds.

A week's leave was granted, so Arthur Barrow, Jim Barnes of Accrington, Jack Fildes of Pendleton, Norman Rowe of Sale, Joe Connolly of Stalybridge and Jim, of Huddersfield journeyed north together.

These days passed soon and we were back taking voluminous notes and studying most nights. We were now placed in private billets and Joe Connolly and I were billeted at 35, Bishops Road with Mr and Mrs Scott.

The Scotts run a pleasant household consisting of Mr and Mrs Scott, Mr Scott's mother who had a suite at the top of the house, his brother and fiancee, Mrs Hawkins, an alert lady of eighty, and Mrs Wright an attractive girl whose husband had recently been called up and was in training in the RAF at Skegness.

Mrs Scott was the essence of homeliness, an excellent cook, a pleasant conversationalist, and exceptionally busy lady. Her interests extended from helping in the Forces Canteen at Euston; dressmaking, she had been a theatrical costumier; assisting the Waifs and Strays Society; and making and receiving social calls from her friends who were Poles and Czechs.

Our stay at 35 Bishops Road was most happy. We each

15

had a key and although there was much banter from the household when we arrived back late, no questions were asked.

Cinema shows, concerts and dances were held on the QD once per week and these were exceptionally good affairs. Invitations to dances were showered upon us, the one from the Wrens' establishment in the new London University Building being always accepted. On these occasions Joe, Scotty of Northampton and Hanford and I invariably went together.

On Saturday night I usually went to the West End, or danced at the Astoria in Covent Gardens. Jack Baird of Edinburgh and Arthur Cadman also came. The jitterbug was the craze, having been made popular by the American troops. The high speed stepping of this dance was fascinating, and was something I never mastered.

I became ill with tonsilitis and was placed in the Sick Bay for a week. My stay here was much enlivened by the Sick-bay Tiffy, a typical Lancastrian from Church. Captain Woodhouse also came to visit me, such was the caring nature of this officer. Mrs Scott came twice to see me.

I received a delightful present, a dog. He was a cross between an Old English Sheep dog and a Spaniel. He had a shaggy coat, sandy in colour, flap ears, stocky legs, and tufts of hair which drifted over his eyes. His owner was Mrs Oakley, a widow, who lived in the flat next door to Mrs Scott's house. She was unable to keep him any longer in her flat, he was growing up, and in view of her going out to work and the frequent bombings, and her two small children, the question of keeping the dog was becoming worrying. I took him home, with the hope that he would be accepted, on a week-end leave. He was idolised by the passengers on the train. The family decided to keep him somewhat relunctantly at first as he misbehaved during the night. I left him with them and returned to London. I called him Dusty. He lived for thirteen years and charmed not only the family but everyone who saw him. He had such a friendly nature. I never took a better present home.

On Sunday Joe would attend Mass at St Joseph's and I went to Jackson's Lane Methodist Church just around the corner, or to Archway Central Hall. At the first mentioned church I was invited to call on the Perrys who worshipped there but I was never able to accept the invitation. Mr Perry and his wife sang in the choir, and were related to Lord Perry. I had tea with the minister Rev. Burton, in the vestry. In his younger days he was minister of Miles Platting Methodist Church, in the next district to the one in which I lived.

During my stay in London I joined the Queensbury Services Club which had use of the London Casino. It was open daily, and during the evenings you could dance on the stage. Geraldo's Sextet usually provided the music. Marvellous shows were staged on Sunday nights, the best London stars appearing.

One very pleasant day at *President V* was Sports Day. The sun shone brilliantly, the racing was good, and afternoon tea served on the lawns gave one the impression of being at a public school.

All good things come to an end and so did the course at Highgate. I came third in the examinations. I think I could have done better but I had missed the lectures whilst in sick-bay. My Divisional Officer, Lt. Colvin recommended me for a commission and Lt. Compton also supported this. Captain Woodhouse sent for me and suggested that I stay for another ten weeks and study the other half of the Accountancy course, the Secretarial side. I thanked him but stated I wished to go to sea as soon as possible. He acceded to my request, and recommended me for a commission.

A farewell of some description had to be held but what kind of celebration? Our difficulties were solved by Scotty's landlady who threw a party for his friends. Joe, Scotty, Hanford, Ray Cooper, another rating whose name I cannot remember, were invited. Before the party we went to the

Golders Green Empire and caused much mirth and commotion of a pleasant kind, for the audience around us.

We journeyed rather noisily back to Southdown Road where a magnificent evening was spent in a whist drive, singing, and supper. Of course female company was provided. Supper was superb, more so because these were the days of rationing. The mahogany table reflected the soft lights and the piled dishes of chicken sandwiches, pasties, sausage rolls, trifle (made with Sherry and a base of caramel) and cakes. We finished the evening with excellent Sherry. This was an evening to remember. Now what about southern hospitality?

On Friday, 9th October, 1942, I left Highgate. Hammocks, kit bags, etc. had been loaded on the ship (lorry). We stood in formation in the yard and received a farewell speech from the Skipper. We gave him a rousing cheer, and one for Jimmy the One, our Divisional Officer, Highgate, and the Navy. As our lorries passed slowly by the ship the remaining classes, with a strong contingent of Wrens to the fore, gave us a terrific send off. Then with Highgate disappearing from our view, we travelled to Waterloo Station, our journey being particularly noisy with songs, shouts to girls, pretty and not so pretty, cat calls and Victory V signs.

We arrived at HMS *Victory*, Portsmouth, after the usual delays at the station and longer one at the ship whilst we went through joining routine. To me, Pompey Barracks appeared grim and forbidding. Huge blocks of buildings surrounded the barrack square which was also the Quarter Deck. Ratings criss-crossed everywhere, all with the air of greatest urgency and total regard for duty, probably assumed except for those going on leave. We waited for a couple of hours during which time nothing happened concerning us, except our grouse that surely the navy ratings ate. Finally we were offered a week-end leave which I readily accepted, and drawing ration tickets, I shot out of HMS *Victory*, drew enough money for my rail ticket from the Post Office, and travelled back to London. I caught the

20.45 from Euston and arrived home at 04.00 on Saturday morning. My entry awakened Dusty whose barks and wagging tail awakened the household. I had not seen him since I had joined up.

I travelled back to Portsmouth on Monday and had to be in before 17.30. On my arrival I was given a draft chit to HMS *Formidable* which I learned was an Aircraft Carrier.

On Tuesday 13th October I went through joining and drafting routine. The MO was not satisfied with my state of health and before he would pass my draft to *Formidable* he obtained a separate opinion. Most likely it was possibly a result of tonsilitis. I passed O.K. It was whilst awaiting the results of my medical report that I met A.E.M. West, one of the solicitors from the place where I worked. He was in matelot uniform which did not compare with the immaculate appearance he always had in Civvy Street. It was working uniform.

There was a great number on draft, all travelling north. Three of us, PO Steward Daniels, W/TJ Pilling and myself were for *Formidable*, but where she lay no one knew. At Waterloo the party divided, some for Euston and some for King's Cross. Kit was thrown into two lorries, one for each station. In view of everyone's ignorance as to where our ship lay, Jack Pilling's and my luggage were placed in the wrong lorry, a fact which we did not discover until we found no meal had been provided for us at Euston. I suggested to the PO in charge that I should go over to King's Cross and find out whether we should be with that party. He suggested that we should travel up to Glasgow with him, and if the *Formidable* were not there perhaps we could find out where our ship was. I didn't think much of his idea, and persuaded him to let me go to King's Cross and find out what they knew. No doubt the PO was worried that I might abscond. At King's Cross the PO was in a flat spin; he discovered that two members of his draft were missing, despite the fact that two meals had not been eaten. Jack and I hurried back to Euston only to find Jack's belongings had been removed. We found them at last and with the help of

19

the RTO's van we got to King's Cross and snatched a hurried meal at the Salvation Army Caledonian Canteen. The others had dined at the Union Jack Club. We entrained for Inverkeithing. At Edinburgh we breakfasted at the YMCA and caught the next train from Waverley Station. We crossed the Firth of Forth Bridge. Shipping of all description could be seen below.

It was raining when we reached Rosyth. There was the usual bustle of a dockyard, its untidiness hit you, the whole aspect was depressing. For the first time I saw destroyers, cruisers, ML's etc., and their size disappointed me. I had expected something much bigger. At last the *Formidable* hove in view. The sight was forbidding. I walked gingerly over the brow, complete with hammock, kit bag, etc. and found myself in a labyrinth. I was bewildered.

I attended the Pay Office, Captain's Office, MO etc. and then was escorted to Mess 15. I needed a friendly guide. Ladders appeared everywhere, passages lead to goodness knows where, or nowhere. I was certain the ship's designers were sadists, or they suffered from nightmares. I was sure I would never find my way round the ship, a feeling I had for a fortnight.

On the 16th October we left Rosyth at 0800 with the *Nelson* and five destroyers. The Captain cleared the lower deck and informed us that Scapa was our next destination. We arrived at 13.00, but before that I had experienced sea sickness, which lasted fortunately for only five minutes.

Scapa Flow has excellent anchorage. The low surrounding hills appear to be covered with pleasant pasturage dotted here and there with small farmsteads. Many ships were in including the *Howe, Anson* and *K.G.V.*

We left harbour at 10.00 on the 18th for landing practice for 893 Squadron, which had arrived at 16.30. During the stay the army fired a deafening barrage over the fleet.

On the 19th Action Stations were exercised. In the Servery Flat, my job was Ammunition Supply Assistant.

20

Four in a team worked on a bomb hoist, the bombs were brought up from the decks below, where the Magazines were, by conveyer belt. The hoist was controlled by a foot pedal, the bombs being lifted on to a small platform. We then carried the bombs to rollers which conveyed the bombs to the gun turrets. The hoist had a Teleflex system by means of which you signalled the type of bomb you required from the Magazine, e.g. S.A.P., H.A., R.D.F.Star.

You wore anti-flash gear at action stations consisting of a hood, mask, gloves, your trousers were tucked into your socks. The heat was unbearable, the atmosphere very stuffy which did not help matters considering the amount of clothing and anti-flash gear which were essential for our protection.

Obviously something was afoot. We were being trained to know exactly what our jobs were from A to Z and at the same time to get us accustomed to actual fighting conditions. What to do and where to go in the event of the ship having to be abandoned were drilled into us. We wore our life belts at action stations ready to inflate them should the necessity arise, and our respirator was in close proximity.

At Scapa the ship was listed at 15 degrees. We were at our action posts and it was a peculiar feeling to walk the decks at this angle. Abandon Ship Stations were piped and we hurried to the flight deck and took up our positions. We were marched in all directions over the flight deck in order to get the feel of the ship with a list and give us confidence in the capabilities of the ship.

At 13.00 on the 24th October we left Scapa and arrived at Greenock at 20.00. This was the first time I had sailed through the Isles. I had mentioned this to the mess president, L.S.A Killey from Rochdale, expressing regret I would miss the beauty of the voyage because of darkness. He was on watch at the time but phoned down to tell me we were passing through and there was good light from the moon. I went to the weather deck. The placid water, the

Coolins rising dark and sombre, the reflections in the moonlit sea, and the steady motion of the ship made it an hour to savour.

The 25th was apent in landing practice for the Seafires. Unfortunately one was lost and the pilot killed. On the following day another Seafire crashed on the deck, hit the barrier, but the pilot was safe. Six Seafires landed today and eleven more on the 27th. We arrived back in Greenock on the 27th at 14.00

The 30th saw us off again, but luckily I had managed a shore run. Greenock did not appear very attractive that winter evening. My impression standing in a Cinema queue was of small gangs of boisterous girls and boys parading the streets. I was with P.O. Absolom on this occasion and our wait in the queue to see "The Fleet's In" was much enlivened by the conversation of a recently married couple behind us, a Scots girl and a Dutch sailor. The sordid circumstances of her home life, and the uncertainty of her marriage to a foreigner, were told in a light-hearted manner, touched with poignancy.

At 23.30 we left Greenock in company with the *Victorious* and a few destroyers, meeting en route the *Nelson*, *Rodney* and *Duke of York*. On November 1st we were heading out into the Atlantic. Was it Yankeeland, or the Mediterranean, or where? Buzzes, and more than that, circulated but by November 2nd we were informed of the part we were to play.

I was in the Goffer Bar when the Skipper spoke to us over the broadcast system. The atmosphere was tense. Even the game of uckers stopped. You could hear the crackle of a lighted pipe, or the scratching of a match, greatly magnified in the silence. We were to take part in the North African Campaign, to land troops and establish postions west of Rommel's troops, thereby creating a pincer. In view of the attitude of the French towards the British we would be sailing under the Stars and Stripes. We didn't like that. Old

Glory is a wonderful flag but for us the White Ensign. But we were to do as we were told and Glory flew.

On the 4th November ten destroyers relieved ours for oiling. We were approaching Gibraltar and sailed through the Straits during the cover of darkness. The entrance to the Mediterranean was the cause of much talk of experience by the seasoned crew who had spent eighteen months on Malta Convoys, the hardships, unceasing duties and strain. I had got what I wanted to be at sea and had no feelings on the promise of action and the novelty for me of impending danger.

I went on the flight deck about 0700 on the 6th. We had picked up the convoy and the organisation behind this expedition made one feel proud to belong to the Navy. Assembled within a few hours was the Armada of Armadas; troop ships, battle wagons, cruisers, carriers, banana boats, boats of every description rode the sea. The sight inspired confidence and if Jerry could see it I am sure he would have had fear instilled in him.

Sailing eastwards one could have forgotton that we were at war. The majestic height of the Sierra Nevadas, their snow capped peaks glistening in the warm sun, made you think this was a Cook's Tour, a wish that was soon to be thrown aside and thoughts turned in another direction when one of our destroyers had an argument with a U-boat. The latter was brought to the surface at 09.30, but a transport ship had already been hit and sunk. Our attacks were to be on the North African coast at Oran and Algiers.

At midnight on the 7th our Albacores flew off to drop not bombs, but leaflets over Algiers. These leaflets were printed in French and Arabic containing a message from the President of the United States, whose photograph appeared on the leaflet. They were also headed by the Stars and Stripes and were signed by Dwight D. Eisenhower, Lieutenant General, Commader-in-Chief of the American Forces.

23

We were at Action Stations on the 8th November during which we were informed that flares dropped by enemy planes were illuminating the Fleet. Any moment we could expect a shelling and we wondered why we did not get one. Later it was learned that the flares were not being used to light up the ships for coastal batteries but for the benefit of the packs of submarines all around us who were firing more than sufficient torpedoes to sink all our ships. By good fortune they missed us.

Splendid news came through on the 9th at 0630. The troops had been landed at all points and at 0830 the aerodromes had been taken. Despite the glorification of all troops except the British, it is understood it was the British, marines, matelots and commandoes who were the advance parties and did the graft. The Fort was blown up and the Seafires shot down enemy planes during the day. Enemy bombers again attacked us, this time at 1630. Torpedoes hurtled between the *Victorious* and the destroyer screen. We secured from action stations, however, at 20.00 only to return and re-secure at 00.15. Planes were diving through the barrage the Fleet was putting up, and torpedoes fell just short of us again. The night brought further torpedo bombers and Action Stations.

It was a quiet sensation working at Action Stations. The bombardment was not continual during the whole of the period so during the lull we would lie on the hot steel deck and swelter. It's better being warm and dry, however. Our turret asked for and got over a hundred 84lbs. shells from us in half an hour and believe you me, was I shattered. The chattering sound of the pom-poms told us of diving aircraft. Men lay in wait for immediate action, whilst the three of us carried shells incessantly to a turret with an insatiable appetite. I was thankful when respite came and Harry Rice of Blackpool, Peter Hibbert of London and I, "A" Turret Ammunition Supply Party sank thankfully on the deck and amused ourselves with attempts at scat singing.

Enemy aircraft were still circling on the 10th during the

early hours of the morning dropping flares. HMS *Martin* was sunk. 05.30 and Action Stations again because of a small force of enemy bombers, one of which was shot down by *Victorious*.

Flares were still being dropped around us on the 11th so that enemy submarines could have a lunge at us. HMS *Ibis* was sunk. 17.45 and Action Stations again and sure enough the expected attack by dive and torpedo bombers came. Our Intelligence should be congratulated on the forecasting of the expected time of these attacks. The *Viceroy of India* was sunk and also the Dutch troop ship *New Zealand and HMS Marne*. The enemy are doing too darned well and they are still illuminating us. On the 12th another ship was sunk. Friday the 13th. and the Dutch Destroyer *Isaac Sweer* hit and sunk at 04.45. We're still lucky, two torpedoes passed under our bows and nearly got us again at 10.20. Our look-out has been very hot at spotting torpedo tracks, and two of the look-out have been rewarded out of the Canteen Fund for their vigilance. I'd give them the whole fund. The constant strain of keeping watch in a sea which washes phosphorescent must be wearing, but these lads are good.

14th November. Good news, we're going back to Gibraltar with the *Duke of York*. A sinking submarine was spotted today and four torpedo bombers were ranged for the kill. The submarine managed to beach in neutral territory.

We arrived at Gibraltar at 00.30 on the 15th. The *Isaac Sweer* survivors came aboard and were victualled in our mess. A few of them spoke English and before they left us weeks later we had made good friends.

Rear Admiral Lister came on board on the 16th and in the course of his address assured the Dutch lads that they would soon have the opportunity for revenge as we were leaving again that night. I wonder how they felt. They should have been given passage to the U.K. Sixteen of them managed to get drafted but twelve stayed with us, the sixteen went to the *Victorious*. We put to sea at 10.00. One of our aircraft sank a U-boat today.

The Dutch were a pleasant crowd, and when fully kitted soon settled down. Peter van Pelt we christened "the cockney". He had spent most of his life in the East End of London and was full of perkiness and cockney humour, though his accent was Dutch. A youngster from Johannesburg spoke English as did the steward. A pleasant feature was that the two coloured Dutchmen were quite at home among us and were accepted without any of the fussiness you meet in England. Perhaps that is due to the attitude of the Dutch themselves and explains their excellent colonising powers. Phillipus came from Batavia and had quite a good position in the Nederland Maritime. Most of their time they spent in an intricate card game of patience, played with two packs and requiring two players.

The next few days we spent in going backwards and forwards between Gibraltar and Mers-el-Kebir in Algeria, so much so that we call ourselves the ferry boat. On the 22nd the only event of note was our hitting the jetty at Gibraltar. The *Furious* and *Renown* left with us on the 24th together with two cruisers. The sea cut up so rough that on the 25th we did not go into harbour but waited outside MeK for the storm to abate.

On the 26th a tragic incident occurred. Waves swept the Commander of the *Furious* off the mole and he was killed.

Our next job was to cover the *Scylla* and *Charybdis* which were on an operation east of Algiers.

27th November brought thrilling news, the scuttling of the French Fleet at Toulon. The possibility of the Axis utilising this fleet had always been in our minds, but as news came through over the wireless we had very mixed thoughts—admiration for their courage, bitterness that they had not foreseen their own danger and thrown their lot in with us and the Free French. At any rate more of them might have attempted to escape. Bits of information kept coming through but weeks later the high hopes of the complete destruction of this fleet were found to be shattered.

26

We met the cruisers at 16.30 and came again within range of enemy long range torpedo bombers. We were spotted by JU 88s.

November 28th found us east of Bougie and at 11.00 on the 29th we were back at MeK.

Sports were held on the 1st December from 15.00 until dark on the flight deck. Various freak races were held, for example, express relay, chariot, four-legged and Charlie Chaplin events. A most enjoyable day.

There was excitement in depth charging a submarine, this afterwards turned out to be an escaped French submarine from Toulon. Luckily the submarine came unscathed into Oran.

The *Manxman* was hit during the night and limped into MeK with a list to starboard. I went aboard her when she was tied up and pitied the conditions under which the crew exisited on these slanting decks.

At 11.30 on the 4th we left MeK and swept eastwards thence proceeded to Gibraltar. As we were sitting in the mess that night without warning our guns opened up. We raced for our equipment but the episode soon ended. A tin fish had just missed us. Two Albacores were sent off in search of the submarine but their search was unsuccessful. We arrived at Gibraltar at 14.30. Wally Thain and Jock Steward got drafts to the U.K. today.

The *Rodney* and the *Nelson* left with us on the 10th and we anchored in the stream at MeK at 11.00 on the 11th. Aircraft were flown off on the 13th but we were only out at sea for two hours.

HMS *Porcupine* and HMS *Partridge* were sunk on the 17th. Their survivors came aboard and left with the *Empress of Canada* on the 23rd. The ship left again on the 24th with the *Rodney* and *Nelson* but this time Algiers was our destination. We covered two convoys.

December 25th. Christmas Day. Just off again. Algiers

once more. We did not enter harbour as Darlan had been assassinated. We returned to Gibraltar.

The ship's choir sang carols today and Christmas Eve. We attempted a Christmassy look to the mess, the decorations had been bought in Oran. The mess was festooned and paper hats, musical toys and similar nonsensities were in profusion.

The Christmas Fare was first class. We certainly were lashed up and the Galley had excelled themselves.

My thoughts wandered back home and down memory lane: carol parties, dances, socials, Christmas cards set around the house, visits to and by friends, morning service in chapel. A few of us, Bob Cherry, Jack Armstrong and others had our own carol service on a weather deck.

There was an unpleasant incident for me. A communion Service had been piped for the Church of England. Marine Pogson, a Baptist arranged our non-conformist services but duty prevented his being able to arrange a service for us. I approached the chaplain with a view to his allowing me to take part in his service. He informed me that "as a Methodist I had cut myself adrift from the Church and was, therefore, not entitled to any of the church's benefits". Fair enough. I should not have put him in that position but the day prompted me. He then paused and said if I considered the aspect he had pointed out to me and thought I should attend, I may attend, but until the respective churches had settled their differences it was better that I did not attend. I did not attend. I wonder when the unification of the various denominations will be accomplished when our boundaries are so definitely fixed, even in such unusual circumstances as war.

At this time Sing-song arrangements were made to take place in the hangar. A sing-song begins very circumspectly and gradually descends, then rushes, into abysmal crudity.

At 19.30 on the 26th we arrived at Gibraltar and the following day some film stars came aboard.

1943

New Year's Eve. The inhabitants of Oran had given us a goodly supply of local wine and this was dealt out to each mess. I tasted it but found it somewhat unpalatable. There was much merriment on the mess decks this evening. I was determined to see the New Year in and a minute or two before midnight I went up on the flight deck. Only a few ratings had the same idea. Soon the air was rent by the shrill call of many ships' sirens. The harbour echoed and re-echoed. 1943 was here. I went back to the mess, slung my hammock and felt a little disappointed. New Year wasn't the same without Auld Lang Syne and Hail Smiling Morn. I hadn't closed my eyes when my hammock was shaken. On either side of me slung Killey and Aelen, both northerners, Lancashire and Westmorland. We crossed hands from our hammocks and sang Auld Lang Syne, our hammocks swinging in rhythm. And no boots were slung at us. 1943 wasn't going to be so bad after all.

The Ensa Concert Party I had seen at the Theatre Royal entertained the ship's company on New Year's Day 1943. I did not see the show as I was on duty at the Victualling Yard.

We left Gibraltar the following day with the *Furious*, *Renown* and *Nelson* and destroyers and escorted a convoy to Algiers. Again we were unlucky as although we had tied up no leave was possible, so back again to the Rock arriving there at 17.00 on the 5th.

Another week at Gibraltar and again the company of the *Rodney* and *Nelson* to MeK. Whilst at MeK the *Ajax* which had been hit by dive bombers came into harbour late in the afternoon of the 13th.

On January the 17th the ship's Concert Party entertained the crew. It was entertaining to see the antics of Basil Dorset and Chris Whyatt, two members of the mess and Martletts

Dance Band attempting to tie bow ties. Finally Ray Layton came to their rescue only to be enmeshed in the operation. My throat was troubling again, the mess was empty, so I made a hot drink of lemon juice, slung my hammock and retired. I had just reached a terrific sweat when the red warning sounded. I jumped out smartly from the hammock and donned overalls. I believe the hangar audience disappeared in a second. The traffic outside our mess door sounded like a local Derby in Manchester and every moment another messmate spewed into the mess. The white sounded immediately. I climbed into my hammock.

Until this time I had not seen aircraft catapulted off the flight deck so on the 20th I had the time to remedy this omission. Dodger Long was of the same opinion so together we climbed to a good vantage point way up on the island, known as goofers' viewing point. We lay there watching the aircraft come up by the lift well, the Fleet Air mechanics and aircraft handling parties pushing the planes into position. The air was still, the moon shed a soft light over the bay. Suddenly a drone of an aircraft was heard and an enemy plane dived out of the moon, and dropped an unwelcome load. Pom-poms opened up and shattered the night air. The flight deck might have opened up and swallowed the ratings working there such was the rapidity with which it was cleared. Dodger and I were still scrambling down from the island when the bombs crashed near the crane just missing the ship. The excitement finished at 21.30.

More American troops were arriving. Their comments were typical—"You can go now" was a favourite one. They calmed down afterwards.

5th February was the day for the regatta. The weather was rough but cutters and whalers were pulled. The Accountants' crew won their heat putting up the fastest time. A Tote was held and I backed the Marines, but in navy parlance, "They let me down."

We left harbour on the 7th with the *Rodney, Nelson, Adventure* and an escort of destroyers. Help was sent to a merchant ship which had been attacked. A tin fish just missed one of our destroyers but otherwise the journey back to Gibraltar was uneventful and we arrived on the 8th.

We were troubled by a JU 88 on the 10th but it was flying too high to hit.

On the 12th the *Rodney* and *Nelson* left harbour at 20.00 with destroyers and cruisers leaving us the only large ship at the Rock.

A grand boxing competition, Ship's Company versus the Black Watch was held, the *Formey* won 13—11. I managed to see the last two bouts hanging from the bulkhead.

The next few weeks were spent at Gibraltar. The Rock consists of Main Street with short streets running off, whilst ramps and stepped streets connect to King Edward Road. Main Street is full of shops where you could purchase, sufficient money being available, silks, Spanish, Moroccan, and Oriental articles etc. It was always thronged with matelots.

On passing through Ragged Staff Gate I usually turned left and wound my way through Southport Gate by which lay Trafalgar Cemetery, the resting place of those who died of the plague which occurred in the 19th Century. Sometimes I turned right and climbed to the top of the Rock. Many times Bert Chandler, Jack Aelen and I obtained a lift in an army lorry which would take us to Windmill Flats. From here we would climb the rest of the way, passing the barracks en route. On one occasion a soldier lent us binoculars and we got splendid views of Algeciras, La Linea, and Catalan Bay.

We climbed down the other side where the white outcropping reminded me of Derbyshire. In doing so we saw one of the Rock apes prowling around. This prompted the usual discussion as to how the apes came to the Rock, whether there was a secret tunnel to an island in the

Mediterranean and would it ever be found, and also the saying that when the apes leave Gibraltar the British Empire would fall. An army hut perched in a crevice had the inscription "Martin's Mountain Goats." It was good to rest on one of the shelves and watch the huge air liners landing at North Front.

By now our appetites had been whetted. There was a good selection of dining places from which to choose. The Imperial Tea Rooms had a definite English appearance, here were afternoon tea and cakes. At the Britannia in College Lane steak, egg and chips with a huge hunk of bread was always worth eating. Another time we might go to the Granada which was not too clean but had a Spanish atmosphere; waiters at the double, animated conversations among the diners, swarthy Spaniards, and dishes which were distinctly foreign.

The Winter Gardens was also another rendezvous and here for 3s 4d. an excellent four-course dinner could be obtained. The food was delicious and professionally served. It also had a hall where dances were held, there were no females in attendance but brown hatters were the substitute. I was highly amused, I regret to say, by the simpering poses of these males who appeared prosperous. They were elegantly dressed in faultlessly cut suits of expensive material, and they had a good taste in shirts and neckwear. Their peroxided and waved hair, plucked eyebrows, enamelled faces, pointed shoes, were grotesque. The manner in which they smoothed their trousers upon sitting down was comical, and their girlishness on being asked to dance was entertaining. One of them was most indignant at the caperings of a slightly inebriated and attentive but merry matelot. He looked down his nose at him and caused us to knock our drinks over. The fact that two British pongoes were part of this abnormal community seemed lowering and we began to wonder how he had obtained a stripe, was it power of command, though obviously not military.

A feature of Gibraltar was the bars, which had Ladies'

Bands. The bar windows were open and the latest tunes could be heard far down the street. At the Trocadero solo Spanish dances were performed by senoritas. They are always thought to be extremely beautiful but these could not compare with the English girl. Perhaps I had not seen the best. Edward Falquero's cafe, Governor's Parade, was also a favourite spot. Although not lavishly furnished, its green and yellow tables and chairs had a fresh appearance, and the food was also good. From a table near the door you looked across Governor's Square to St. Andrew's Presbyterian Church, white walled, cool and refreshing.

The English Cathedral was in Moroccan style which seemed to fit in with the surroundings more so than the Roman Catholic Cathedral which was a very handsome building.

I visited the Museum and was conducted over the Governor's House. This house had a lovely garden with trees hundreds of years old and lemon and orange trees. The flower beds were not yet in bloom. The Governor, Sir. H. MacFarlane, spoke a few words to our guide, the Rev. Ogilvie of St. Andrew's, and to us visitors.

Each night the Ceremony of the Keys takes place. A small contingent of soldiers, preceded by a band and followed by mounted officers, marches down Main Street to the Casements and afterwards returns by the same route.

Sometimes we would watch a football match on the R.N grounds or visit the R.N. Cinema. Here vendors of oranges, figs, bananas, grapes and salted almonds did a roaring trade. If I were ashore on Sunday I would attend the Methodist Chapel high up on Prince Edward Road. It was built in true Methodist style and its congregation was made up of soldiers, sailors, and airmen. The chapel was founded in 1769 and on the wall is a tablet which reads:

> To the Glory of God and in sacred Memory of Sergeant (afterwards Ensign) Henry Ince of H.M. 2nd Foot, in whose House, standing on this site the first Methodist Services in Gibraltar were held, and the Methodist Society found a Home.
> 1769—1804.

Before the evening service on Sunday the congregation would choose the hymns to be sung before the service began. On Tuesdays a Christian Endeavour meeting was held. The one I attended was packed and was exceptionally good. The history of the chapel makes compelling reading. The early connection with Methodism is the soldiers and sailors garrisoned on the Rock. From time to time there was persecution of the members depending on the views of the Governors. General Lord Cornwallis ordered that they should not be molested or their meetings disturbed.

On Nelson's flagship bands of praying men were found, and Nelson himself ordered that they should have a mess to themselves and not be interfered with in their worship. A certain Major-General Barnett forbade the men to preach or attend Methodist services on pain of court martialling. For this crime two corporals were reduced to the ranks and received 200 lashes each, the others charged were sentenced to 500 hundred lashes each which was forgiven but would be put into practice if they were found attending such meetings.

At one time the authorities had a civilian posted on the door to prevent any one entering. In 1832 burial was refused to the body of a soldier's child because it had been baptised by a Wesleyan minister. London was approached which resulted in a special portion of the cemetery being set aside as a Wesleyan Burial Ground. There were other events but those mentioned will be enough to show the determination of men in the past to have religious freedom.

I liked the appearance of Gibraltar from the basin. Terraced houses hugged the base of the Rock and the twinkling lights at night gave it a theatrical look. At night from the top of the Rock a searchlight stabbed the sky and silhouetted the Rock.

At 21.00 the bars closed and their customers spilled into the streets unsteady of gait and loud with song. Naval pickets marched up and down. Their H.Q. was the Naval Picket House near Southport Gate.

I have mentioned previously the Ensa Concert given on the ship on New Year's Day. I saw this show at the Theatre Royal near Governor's Square. The theatre has a broad flight of steps which gives it a distinctly foreign aspect. The artists at the show were John Gielgud, Beatrice Lillie, Edith Evans, Michael Wilding, Jeanne de Casalis, Phillis Stanley, and Elizabeth Welch.

On the 11th March we went to sea again leaving the Rock at 13.30 but soon returned at 19.30. We exercised Action Stations.

We left again on the 12th for MeK. We ran into a storm, lightning illuminated the sea which danced to the flashes. We arrived at MeK in stormy weather. I heard Deep Harmony being played by a brass band over the wireless and this aroused many thoughts of home.

Over the Tannoy on the 15th we were given an account by a member of the ship's company, who was there, of the raid on St. Nazaire. The part played by the Atherstone, Tynecastle, Campbeltown and M.L.134 was graphically described: the encounter with a submarine; the approaches down the mouth of the Loire; coastal guns firing at point blank range; the landing of commandoes and the blowing up of important buildings; and the return without that promised air support were wonderfully told.

March 16th and shore leave again. Bert Chandler, Jack Allison and I set off for Boisieville, or Ain el Turck. We enjoyed this sea side resort, apparently the summer resort of the wealthy Oran people. It has a pleasant beach sheltered by high sand dunes. Many modern villas, which were not inhabited, as it was winter, fringed the coast. They were mostly flat roofed, cubist in design and superbly coloured. It was like a Hollywood film set.

We climbed into a villa through a window and deposited our clothes in a wardrobe before going for a swim. The houses were excellently appointed; electric light, showers, bath, sun terraces and other modern conveniences made them wonderful holiday apartments. Unfortunately vandalism was taking effect. Small Arab youngsters emerged from these deserted villas. They had obviously been on a foraging expedition.

Arab settlements lay away from the beach, rudely constructed but interesting. Veiled women drew water from a well, swarthy Arabs were ploughing fields, tethered goats and cattle munched away. There were flowers in profusion, pine groves, and the lovely, low but wide spreading branched almond trees which looked as they had been covered in hoar frost. All these gave a Biblical touch to the scene. On the road we met Arabs riding slowly on mules or trudging in their camel-skin heel-less slippers.

The rugged coast line with rocky coves reminded me of Cornwall and the coast road became a favourite walk. Below was the Mediterranean Sea, its colour changing from deep blue to green, indicating the shallow and deep parts.

Sometimes we would climb the hills where a magnificent view of the harbour was obtained. The look-out was superb, ships lying motionless in the bay, glimpses of tall buildings of Oran peeping behind Santa Cruz.

Oran is a modern city with wide boulevards, excellent shops, fine buildings. Many American, Free French and French Legion troops were here.

I was determined to try most things and although the long queues of Americans, matelots and marines, outside the bay shanties, left me astonished, I came to accept them. I did try the 'Blue' Pictures, but the crudity was nauseating and made more than one matelot vomit in the fresh air outside.

St. Patrick's Day. We began the day with Irish songs being played over the wireless and sung also by us during breakfast time. Bedding had to be aired today. Mine became soaked. I was working six decks below alone and no pipe penetrated down there, consequently I did not hear that it was raining and to bring in your bedding. I was blissfully unconscious that my bed, hammock, blanket etc were fluttering in the wet wind, Jock Cruikshank, however, came to my rescue and dried my belongings in his store.

On the 19th again shore leave and Bob Cherry and I went again to Boisieville. The sun blazed down, sun bathing and swimming were delightful. Two Texan soldiers were on the beach so we all went to the Bar Vincent where the muscatel was refreshing.

Sunday the 21st and another march past. This time Admiral Willis took the salute. He explained the changes in the command of Force H, the appointment of Admiral Syfret to a high post in the Admiralty and the temporary appointment of Admiral Burrows pending the return of Admiral Willis from the East.

The weather was still glorious and I managed a little sun bathing in the dinner hour. During the night I was called out to supply the *Halcombe* with bread. Fortunately the M.L. drew alongside and their hands hauled the stores inboard.

Great activity this evening. A merchant ship was attacked off Oran during the night and an oiler was torpedoed. Alarm to arms was sounded about 0100 and depth charging continued. There was great U-boat activity outside and danger of human torpedo attacks.

German and Italian prisoners were escorted along the jetty to the adjoining American troopship.

More panic on the night of 23/24. This time there were human torpedo attacks but our jetty patrol saw them off. Pom-poms and depth charges disturbed the night but Action Stations lasted for only an hour. Italian submarines were in the vicinity and one had fired on an Albacore on A.S.P.

Once again we left and returned to Gibraltar arriving on the 26th. Lower Deck was cleared on the 27th and a letter from Admiral Cunningham was read. This was in relation to drunkenness at Gibraltar and that in the future this would be regarded as an aggravated offence. I thought the assembly would be in relation to food as I had ditched three of my dinners that week.

Sunday the 28th. Bert Chandler and Jack Allison who had got a draft to U.K. chit and I went ashore to gannet. I had eggs and a double portion of chips. Big licks for grandad! Afterwards we saw a splendid show at the Theatre Royal performed by the Services including four Wrens. The play was "Noah's Ark" and was excellently produced and acted. I sympathised with the players, apparently only a strip tease would meet with approval. Catcalls and unintelligent comments were frequent. Noah, a terrific performance, said at the fall of the curtain, "If some of you have enjoyed the play, thank you, to others Goodnight."

Wednesday we went to sea for flying exercises. F.O.H. Admiral Willis and the Governor of Gibraltar came on board. There were twelve catapult launches, one hundred and eleven deck landings (one crumple) and 217 ons and offs. A practice shoot was held at night and star shells fired. Practice torpedo attacks were made.

April 2nd and shore leave. I had intended having a decent meal and doing a show but met Steve and Charlie. We decided on one drink and then eats. The drinks increased because others joined us. Finally we got away and dined at the Winter Gardens, finishing with excellent sherry. I did know my way back to the ship and remember that I was crooning contentedly.

We left Gibraltar for Oran but strange to say we didn't stay long. On Sunday the Skipper told us that we were leaving for Algiers. Apparently the Italians had begun registering all small craft, the obvious reason the evacuation of Rommel's troops from Tunisia. This might mean the possibility of the Italian Fleet's sailing and our being required for action. Enemy activity at Algiers had been persistent. We sailed on Monday and went to Action Stations at 20.20. Enemy aircraft was spotted but we were not troubled. Action Stations again at 06.00 on the 6th and we opened fire on unidentified aircraft. Later it was learned to be a Beaufighter!

We arrived at Algiers at 08.00 on the 6th April. It appeared to be a very clean city. Tall white buildings covered the hillsides and there were well wooded spaces. The Casbah, the native quarter, looked intriguing. It is said that once you have taken refuge there you will not be found. I can well believe it, the flat roofed dwellings nearly touch each other so that you can jump across the space between . No shore leave for me, I must try and change my watch. This time, however, I was stand-by to take notes for an Inquiry, a job I had done previously. Actually this work should have been done by the C.P.O. Writer but he seems to be conveniently engaged. I'm a right Jonah's bastard. The previous case I reported was very interesting, a signal offence about a ship's movement. This Inquiry was conducted by the Skipper and was attended by various officers, and the Jaunty who read the charge, and marshalled the witnesses. This interest will wane unless I am relieved of some of my other duties as I am working longer hours than most.

Many days have elapsed and I have not been able to keep up the diary. Now it's Easter Sunday. I can see the Rock glistening in the hot sunshine. Exercises have been held in the interim period and three kites and two pilots are now no more. The toll is heavy. In accordance with naval custom the effects of the dead were auctioned and in one case £275 was realised. The generosity of the matelot is boundless. Articles are bought and immediately put back in the auction. Perhaps £5 is bid for a dirty, tattered towel which is immediately handed back. This scene is multiplied, nobody wants the articles, yet bidding is feverish.

Interspersed with the heavy storing of the ship I managed a run ashore and saw "Desert Victory", a documentary record of General Montgomery's splendid campaign in North Africa.

On Good Friday and Easter Sunday I attended services at

Providence Chapel, these were church parades. On our way we passed two contingents of the Black Watch who were marching, preceded by a Pipe Band, to the ships waiting to take them back to U.K. Their sun-tanned faces were happy. Three years on the Rock and now U.K., no wonder. The latest buzz is that we are to take them home. Hope springs eternal in the human breast. Everlastingly we are escorting this, that and the other to the U.K. Everlastingly the *Furious, Illustrious, Argus* and *Unicorn* are on their way to relieve us and all that happens is that we sail Cunningham's pond. Again and again someone says, "Next time at Gibraltar we are going home."

This is monotonous: We left Gibraltar with the fleet on the 28th April and arrived MeK at 10.30 on the 30th. The stay was uneventful but soon we were on our way to Algiers and arrived on the 5th May. Admiral Cunningham came on board and we had the indispensable march past. The Admiral was red faced and of average size. He spoke of the months of waiting the Navy had to endure and the hope of the Italian Fleet's venturing to sea. We left Algiers at 20.30 on the 5th and, you've guessed it, arrived at the Rock on the 7th. The *Rodney* left us but the K.G.V. was waiting in dock. I met Norman Hardy who was at Skegness with me.

Nothing of importance to report until the 25th when an Ensa Concert Party entertained us. No important names but it was one of the best shows I've seen. I watched it from the bulkhead ladder and for my trouble had to dhobi the oil-stained clothing afterwards.

The *Howe* came in on the 25th to relieve the *Nelson* which left on the 26th. The *Unicorn* also arrived.

The *Formidable* for the next few days became a film studio. Michael Powell the director of 49th Parallel with Ralph Richardson the stage and screen star, and a number of cameramen were completing a film called "Volunteer" which was about the Fleet Air Arm. Of course, we had to put to sea for exercises and filming but we were back again on the 28th. Many troopers were in on the 29th, and the *Unicorn* left. For us back to sea on the 30th for exercises with *K.G.V.* and *Howe* for 14" shoots. Algiers saw us again on the 1st June, the Glorious First of June.

I was fortunate that I managed a few hours leave in Algiers going ashore at 17.00. Ken Shackleton and I climbed the easterly headland to visit "Notre Dame d'Afrique". It has a commanding view and as you stand by the front entrance there is an uninterrupted view of the sea below you. The church is remarkable for two reasons at least: it has a Black Madonna and is open for worship for Musselmen and I understand, Protestants. We also visited the New Mosque which in fact dates from the the 14th century, although the snow white walls belie its age. I asked in my tin pot French whether we could go inside and what regulations there would be.So long I kept my cap off and did not smoke all would be well I was told. I walked across the stepped street and through the side entrance. Here, of course, crouched the ubiquitous beggars, blind and not so blind.

It was fairly light inside and on the floor were many carpets. An ornate pulpit was situated in the centre of the building; there was a balcony where the women worshipped, the congregation being separated. Many Musselmen were at prayer each appearing to have brought his own mat on which to pray. They were in all positions, some reclining, some squatting, some standing upright as if in a trance, others knelt or prostrated themselves frequently banging their heads on the deck.

We left on the 2nd June and arrived at MeK, where else, on the 3rd. On the whole the weeks had been monotonous, interspersed with occasional runs ashore but no leave. This feeling of frustration, mixed with boredom, perhaps resulted in an extraordinary week. The ship organised picnics for us. Many had been working between decks and getting little or no fresh air and consequently, the whole of the ship's company in watches had a day's outing at MeK. We lined up on the jetty at 08.00 with a Marine Band playing us to the dockyard gate. We marched the few miles to Boisieville. Our meals were brought by lorry. All day long we bathed and sun bathed, taking al fresco dinner and tea under what shade we could find. Lime juice was served before we made our own way back to the ship having to be on board by 18.30. The weather was glorious, the picnic perfect. Good thinking someone.

June 10th and at sea this time for exercising 826 Squadron which had come on board. We had the misfortune of an Albacore crashing in the sea loaded with depth charges. We returned at 16.45. We left again on the 14th with the *K.G.V.* and for some reason the Skipper spoke to us that night. After silence for many months we thought we were going home. Of course the buzzes of the knowledgeable ones were loosening up. All we were told that sailing instructions for U.K. had been in his possession on three occasions and each time they had been countermanded. All we could hope for, in the Skipper's own words, was "when a carrier worthy of us arrived in this area we could look forward to homeward bound."

I should have mentioned that the first run ashore in Algiers was unusual and perhaps should not be broadcast. A number of us sauntered, for want of a better word, as we did not know anything about the town. We had no plan except see as much as possible. We followed a crowd of service men into a building of elegant appearance. Inside was an expansive open floor with steps leading up to a balcony running all round this high and wide room. The architecture was Moroccan with lovely mosaics on the wall. It was a brothel. We went up to the balcony and watched the milling crowd below. Doors of cubicles on the ground floor would open and a satisfied client would leave with a smile and a wave of the hand from the scantily attired hostess. She would then with élan welcome the next hungry pleasure-seeking solicitor. One hostess left her cubicle and crossed the floor fending off amorous attentions on the way from prospective clients with this cryptic remark, "I'm finished for the morning, I've had forty," and she was quite jubilant about her day's work. I was still on the balcony minding my own business when arms encircled my shoulders. I turned round. Holding me was an old timer, past her best in shape and beauty. Perhaps she had been relegated to the upper regions out of the way of the younger dianas. My attention and intention were invited. I replied in my best schoolboy French, "Non merci, mademoiselle, demain, je suis fatigue." With venom she spat out the reply, "Bullshit." Jimmy and Max were rolling about with laughter, they had set me up for this endearing moment. Who requires enemies when you have pals like that?

We were back again. It was the 15th and Gibraltar. The *Howe* arrived from Algiers. We learned that the King was visiting North Africa.

Captain Bissett, the old Skipper, came on board on the 19th when we left with four destroyers. Wonder of wonders we went through the straits into the Atlantic, something which we all believed to be impossible as it was out of bounds.

On June 21st, we met up with the Fleet: *Nelson*, *Rodney*, *Valiant*, *Warspite*, and sixteen destroyers, and the *Indomitable*. During this period we sailed 250 miles from Gibraltar to the westward. The Skipper spoke again to us on the 22nd giving us particulars of the Fleet and the exercises we had made. *Formidable* had shot down the sleeve and had put up the best performance. He said we expected to arrive in Gibraltar the following day, that *Formidable* was to enter the harbour first tying up at the Sheerlegs, and that we were the senior ship in Force H. We were then informed that we were only 800 miles from the U.K. I wonder if passports will be necessary for our entry.

We were told of Operation Torch, the North African Campaign, the tremendous work the Fleet Air Arm had done in accomplishing the troop landings which would not

43

have been possible without the FAA upon which complete cover depended, and that the RAF did not take over until the afternoon when Tafarouia Airfield was captured.

At this time Joe Connolly who was billeted with me at Highgate came aboard. Joe had been drafted to the *Battler,* an American built carrier. Since leaving *President V* he had served at Lee on the Solent, Northern Ireland and Scotland. Only recently he had been drafted to a sea going ship and that they were going back again to the U.K. immediately.

He had had plenty of leave and was expecting a long one on his return. It's how the cookie crumbles, and good luck!

27th June and more exercises. We were piped out of the harbour by four pipers of the Royal Scots who had come aboard early in the morning. They were stripped of their kilts and rigged as seamen. As one had a moustache this led to trouble. Apparently the Skipper had been dining with the Governor of Gibraltar the previous evening and a bet had been made as to our being piped out to sea by matelots. The story went that the *Indomitable* had a bandmaster with flying staff, so we must go one better. The affair was interesting and they played on the flight deck that night to the ecstatic delight of the Scots on board.

29th June. Leave cancelled and we went to sea with *Valiant, Warspite* and eight destroyers.

On the 30th we were informed we were making for Alexandria and should arrive there on Monday the 5th July. The few days at sea passed quickly and, although it was only coastal scenery which we passed, we could see the places made famous by the British Army: Tunis, Tripoli, Cape Bon, Pantellaria, Bizerta, Mersah Matruh, Bug-Bug, and scores of those places which the Drang nach Osten had taken only to their being surrendered.

Shore leave was heaven. Bob Cherry, Basil Biagott, Jock Cruikshank and I joined up and explored the native quarter and haggled in the open shops where marvellous leather work was on sale: sandals, handbags, shoes, suit cases etc. Street vendors were persistent salesmen and it invariably happened that after telling them their prices were too high we were asked how much did we wish to pay? Our prices were always too low, but the fun was good. We then entered a marvellous shopping area: jewellery, leather goods, swim wear, and a host of excellent and fashionable articles were in profusion. First class cafés and hotels with an abundance of appetising food were everywhere. Just as Gibraltar had barber shops at every turn Alexandria had tailor shops. Shopping and sightseeing took up all our time so as hunger assailed us we made for the Fleet Club. These Canteens are usually flyblown and depressing, ill lit make-shift affairs, full of bustling matelots hungry and thirsty and with little time to eat properly. This club was different and exceptional. It was spacious and wonderfully appointed: theatre, dining hall, soda fountain, shops, etc. We had a perfect meal and finished with real ice cream, not Algerian frozen water, and fresh fruit. Native waiters attended to our wants efficiently and with a smile. Jack here was not the despised gutter snipe, but a human being. To sit at a table and eat off clean and delicate crockery, to sit back and enjoy our meal at leisure was wonderful. Josephine Baker was appearing in one of the shows but our appetite for sight seeing had not been satisfied so we missed the show. In the dimness, for the city had a black out, we walked around and along the cool promenade where open air cafés and pavement eating places gave a continental touch. There were attractive Egyptian girls to be seen in smart clothes. There is a strong Italian and Greek population in Alexandria. Eventually we found ourselves, or lost ourselves, in a labyrinth of streets near the docks and with the help of a policeman found our way back. This is no place to be in after dark on your own, even the gharry and taxi drivers are not always to be trusted. Natives lounge at street corners. They squat, lie, sit or assume any position you can imagine, at frequent intervals, whilst their queer sounds and strange tongue add to the mystery of the place.

45

The docks were still busy even at this late hour. Gangs of busy natives heaved heavy loads to dismal chanting which, I was told, was a prayer to Allah to give them strength. Judging by the size of their burdens they certainly needed it.

At sea again on the 7th and heading westwards. This apparently was the beginning of the offensive. Captain Talbot was promoted to Rear Admiral on the 8th.The Fleet was growing, we joined with the *Indomitable, Gert and Daisy, Penelope, Aurora, Cleopatra*. Ships everywhere, two thousand ships and five thousand aircraft.

On July 9th the invasion of Sicily commenced. Paratroops, Airborne troops, and the usual beach landing troops were successfully carried to Sicily. Our job was to provide cover. Hours were spent at Action Stations, morning and night.

Syracuse was captured on the 11th.

On the 12th we put into Malta for a few hours. Our course for the next few days lay between Malta and Sicily, in circles, squares, ovals, and all manner of courses were steered. A request to bomb Catania came but we were not able to arrive there in time. In the meantime we, the ammunition supply party, sweated for hours bringing the 250 lbs. bombs for the flight deck from the magazines, only to return them to the museum the following morning.

Cleopatra was torpedoed and the *Indomitable*, both during the same night. Destroyers stood by the *Cleopatra* and examined the severe damage. The list on the *Indomitable* was righted in ten minutes. The *Indomitable* being hit created the doldrums on board. We had awaited a carrier worthy to relieve us, now this happened. A remarkable thing that Syd our messman, and quite a wag, said when the *Indomitable* joined the force he'd bet she would get hit and so keep us in the Med. I'd prefer to stay out here until the end of the war if that would prevent our being hit.

On the 16th we returned to Malta. We drew alongside the Canteen Quay. That evening the flight deck was crowded. We gazed unbelievably and with sympathy at the shambles of Valetta. Like most ports in this area it is huddled together, terrace rising on terrace in seeming confusion. The yellowish brown buildings looked like a theatre set, cardboard models. But what devastation! It appeared to be a deserted ruin, for surely no one could live in those blasted houses, not one had escaped injury in some way or another. Walls had been rent, roofs had caved in, and here and there an undamaged works chimney stood like a gaunt sentinel over heaps of rubble and crumbled masonry. The ruins of a church on the hillside still kept its belfry and bells, whilst the clock showed bravely, or defiantly, the correct time. Here and there green painted wooden oriel windows clung tenaciously to the blitzed houses.

I went ashore the following day, Saturday, 17th July. All round was complete devastation, although great efforts had been made to clear the mess. The roads were still in good condition or had been re-metalled. The heat of the day and the dazzling whiteness of the landscape suggested our seeking refreshment. We entered a bar and ordered drinks. Those were the only words spoken by Jack Sampson and me. When the bartender did speak all he said, and I can sympathise with him, was, "We had the *Aurora* and *Penelope* (two of our cruisers) here. Those were the only ships and those two ran away when the blitz came." What could we say? Even a rehearsed speech would have been inadequate to console him. There was such a note of pathos in his voice, and grief in his eyes. We swallowed our drinks but did not enjoy them, and mumbled a weak goodbye.

We reached the top of the cliffs by the Barraca Lift and wandered aimlessly round Valetta. St. Paul's Street was a reminder of his shipwreck on this island but leave was short and there was no time for wandering afar to see the spot. A few shops were open and these displayed goods at exorbitant prices; 15s. 0d. for a pair of khaki woollen stockings and 19s. 6d. for a pair of cotton shorts. How the people of this island had suffered and yet they bravely dressed their streets with bunting for the King's visit. Never has a George Medal been so heroically won.

Carrozzias plied the streets and I should have gone sight seeing in one. I believe there are cathedrals on the island but our meanderings took us only to one. Of course, we drifted into the "Gat", the street of noisy bars and their attendant purveyors of vice. Tired, hot and dusty we eventually found the Forces Club, The Vernon. A dance was in progress and the Manchester Dance Band was playing. I spent the rest of the evening there. Down at the quayside crowds were waiting for the liberty boat. As we had to be aboard for 20.00 we hired a dghaisia to take us to the *Formey*. These are gondola like in appearance, some have an awning.

A pongo told us their experiences during the heavy bombardment. Ammunition ran out: they were reduced to six to ten shells a day per gun, and afterwards every other day. Dogs were slaughtered for food. The "All clear" sounded two days after the original siren. There was one plane only to fight against the hordes of Germany and Italy's Luftwaffe. Sixty new Spitfires which had just been landed were wiped out before the crates could be opened. People lived in the catacombs because their homes had disappeared in rubble.

On Sunday, after afternoon tea, it was my turn to empty the gash bucket down the chute into the harbour. It was full of the usual greasy slops, leaves from the tea urn, bits of cake, all swimming round in the dirty washing up water, together with fag ends and other rubbish. Not a pleasant sight. An old man, or did he just look old, was sitting close by the chute. Before I could throw this nauseating junk down the chute, he asked to see it. I put the bucket down. He fished around the filthy dirty stinking mess, and brought out bits of soaking bread, cake, and disgusting particles of what was once food and spread this concoction on a newspaper which quickly stained. I asked, in stupid ignorance, if he were keeping pigs. He looked up from his kneeling position and replied "No, my children." It was worse than humiliation I felt. I could have kicked myself. I then asked him if he liked tinned fish. He brightened up and so did I. I asked him to keep a look-out for my return and quietly indicate if anyone was about by stroking his hair. I returned to the mess. It was empty. For months we had not eaten herrings in tomato sauce, which we had sometimes for our breakfast, because no one liked them. I filled the bucket with as many oval tins as it would hold and covered them with newspaper. I returned to the chute again, it was all clear, and placed the bucket on his spread-out newspaper for him to remove the contents which he did most dexterously into a sack. I made the motion of emptying the gash and returned his grateful smile and thanks.

I made other visits ashore. I managed to get to St. Paul's Bay and saw the statue commemorating St. Paul's shipwreck. I was with Bob Coggins. We swam in the bay, then found there was no bus back to Valetta. We were lucky to have hitch-hiked back passing on the way Moska Cathedral, which has the second largest dome of any in the world. A bomb had crashed through it but had failed to explode. I visited St. John's Cathedral, much damaged but still lovely. The ceiling is wonderfully painted even to shadows of the figures on the roof supports. The walls are intricately hand carved, and the floor is composed of over four hundred slabs marking the resting places of the Knights Templar. The paintings by Michaelangelo and Raphael had been removed for safety, as had the silver gate. This gate on the right of the altar was painted over with a bronze colouring during Napoleon's visit when he was collecting forcibly as much gold and silver as he could to pay for his wars. The ruse deceived him. A bronze gate of similar design is on the left of the altar. We were told of a woven tapestry depicting the Stations of the Cross and made in Belgium over three hundred years ago, which is hung up on St. John's Day, and special occasions such as Eucharistic Conferences. The colour of the tapestry had faded but was in far better condition than a silver curtain in Rome. Many side chapels, the cost of which had been borne by the Knights Templars of many countries, led off from the main body of the church. We paid visits to the Franciscan Church and St. Paul's Shipwreck, which, although beautiful, were not as beautiful as St. John's. The Governor's Palace was also visited. In peace time this would have been interesting but although there were pictures of the history of Malta, the armoury was bare. The Council Chamber and State Rooms were well worth a visit.

Most of our time at Malta was spent swimming at Sliema and St. Julian's Bay with an occasional visit to the open air rendezvous Rockyvale.

We left Malta for Alexandria. I looked at my very much depleted Post Office Savings book and wondered how it could be topped up. Luckily the Paymaster arranged for us to receive part of our month's pay and I sighed, relief was at hand. On 4s. 6d. a day one couldn't lash out frequently.

We went into floating dock to have the ship's bottom scraped. These days are indescribable. No air in the ship, few lights and the heads closed. It was therefore necessary to walk off the ship, complete with cap and station card, in order to go and perform the essential acts of nature. The walk aft and over the gangway, and then forward along the floating dock, would take ten minutes, shorter in cases of immediate urgency, only to arrive at filthy, evil smelling, overcrowded heads, which usually lacked toilet paper, but harboured swarms of flies hovering round the open lavatory bowls. It was here I caught the crabs, such is my blissful ignorance. They burrow into the skin especially round the genitalia and cause intense itching. The remedy was to shave off the affected parts and smother with a special ointment. The worst thing is that you feel disgustingly unclean.

The flies penetrated the ship and it was with the utmost discomfort that we worked. Luckily we were given night leave; it was necessary.

The shops were well stocked. We bargained with sellers of leather, ate ice cream and fresh fruit until we should have been sick, but weren't. We decided on a proper shopping spree but on arriving at Mahomet Ali Square were soon under the spell of a dragoman, who sold us travel (not however, to the U.K.) and sight seeing. First of all he promised iced beer and by devious routes we came to a barber's shop, where iced beer was available. The taxi arrived and soon we were speeding crazily through squalid streets. We came to Pompey's Tower or the Pillar of Diocletian. We looked at this ancient pile fronted by two small sphinxes, and afterwards were escorted to the catacombs. Apparently an early Christian church had existed on this spot. Then we entered more catacombs and the underground resting place of the family of an old Alexandrian lady. The carvings in these catacombs are superb, and the dining hall was exquisite. The date on these ruins was of the time of Alexander the Great.

We shot off to the open air zoo, passing a tributary of the Nile. Admittedly it was very small; it was muddy and you could understand the reason why the plagues had visited Egypt. A large fleet of peculiar flat bottomed boats passed us, laden with grain and swarming with natives. There were lovely parklands ablaze with canna flowers and a profusion of slender palms. Fields of tobacco and sugar beet spread along the road sides. The zoo was delightful; lions sunned themselves, whilst in the next cage tigers trod warily in everlasting circles. I was entranced by the deep black limpid eyes of gazelles. Bears, monkeys, birds of every hue, snakes which hypnotised frogs before eating them, ostriches, besides many other animals appeared to be enjoying life behind bars with the possible exception of the frogs. We hadn't time to see the King's Palace so we took a look at Stanley Bay. Here the bathing is superb and appeared very English. It had taken three hours to cover the ground, so eats were necessary. Justice was done to chicken, steak and chips, omelettes, eggs, fresh fruit and ice cream at the Fleet Club—that was among all of us, not for one. We slept on board, we had to save for another run ashore.

The next run was to be a shopping run. It wasn't. I visited a lovely Greek Orthodox Cathedral. Light and airy, high and wide, it was magnificient. Not a single statue adorned this church, but many icons were visable. The altar is hidden by a huge screen reaching from floor to roof, but a large door in the centre of the screen, is opened at a certain point in the service. We then looked for a mosque and finally entered one. David Chaplin, however, stepped on the mat which reached into the courtyard, still wearing his shoes. We received black looks and the ancient did his best to explain in gesture that an act of sacrilege was being committed. We were loathe to leave our shoes outside so compromised by taking them off and carrying them. I had barely stepped inside the mosque when I felt someone tugging at my shoes from behind me. I was certain I was going to have to walk back to the ship shoeless, for what chance have two matelots among a crowd of natives in a mosque in the native part of the city? It wasn't that bad, I was carrying my shoes wrongly, they had to be carried sole to sole so that, theoretically, no dust would fall on the floor. A few people were on their prayer mats. The floor was completely covered by a carpet. In the centre was a throne-like chair, where the priest would sit and read the Koran and explain the passage to the worshippers who would be sitting at his feet. This mosque was hundreds of years old, we thoroughly enjoyed the visit.

I managed another run ashore and really shopped. I arrived back penniless. I had taken advantage of an all-night leave and slept in an Eygptian hotel. After shopping we dined well, went to the pictures which commenced at 9 pm and finished at midnight. We walked through the dimly lit streets. luckily deserted, finally finding our hotel about 1 am. A number of soldiers were spending their leave there, and even at this time of the morning gargantuan meals were being served. The place was filled with raucous noise, mostly song. A swarthy Egyptian served us with delicious coffee whilst we undressed. He glided about in a flowing robe. I fell asleep about 2 am with the popular tunes of the day still being sung by the soldiers on leave downstairs. Breakfast was served in bed, we were given a gentle shake, no one had heard him enter the room. Hot tea, bread and butter, bacon, eggs, tomatoes, and chips. All for 2s. 0d. Bed and Breakfast.

We arrived at the quay at 06.45 having spent eighteen glorious hours away from the ship. Now we were away and leaving the best place, for me, in the Mediterranean for Malta. Soon the *Illustrious* arrived causing much speculation as to what was afoot. We held exercises with the *Illustrious* and were much impressed by their flying of Barracudas. I tried to contact Norman Taylor, a local lad, in Malta, by way of a change but his regiment had left for Sicily. The invasion of Italy had already commenced across the Straits of Messina and the town of Reggio, occupied with no opposition.

In Malta I saw George Formby and Beryl at Command Fair. His raw humour was appreciated by the large Service audience, but then they were mainly from Lancashire Forces who had held the George Cross Island. George gave encore after encore, even he was dripping with perspiration. He sang Mr Wu, the Air Raid Warden; Fanlight Fanny; It's in the Air; and It serves me right, I shouldn't have joined from his new film Bell-bottom George; and other songs. On Monday Billy Watson another lad from Newton Heath came on board from the the *Illustrious* and we exchanged our local news. On the 7th September we sailed with the huge fleet which had been assembled to cover a combined operation of Great Britain and America to attack Naples, Anzio and Salerno. We were at Action Stations humping shells and pom-pom ammunition through sleepless nights. On Wednesday we were informed that Badolio's Government had agreed to terms of unconditional surrender and that the date of its announcement had been withheld until it was considered opportune. Full instructions had been given to the Italian Fleet to sail to neutral or Allied ports and definite signals had been given them. They were to proceed at 12 knots per hour. Leaflets were being dropped in Italy requesting them to hinder the German communications as much as possible. Deposition of the German forces were known to the Allies, such as the concentration of troops in the heel of Italy, because of the possibility of attacks on Taranto; and the re-forming of the Hermann Goering Division north of Rome; and also the various other troops around Naples and Northern Italy.

Thursday the 10th was a tragic day for mess 15. The youngster of the mess, a bright cheerful S.A. of 18 from Blackpool had kept us amused for the months he was on the ship with his boyish humour. He had a roguish face and smile, a quick temper which subsided immediately, and he bounced in and about the ship. Bernard was an ex-leatherneck, having joined the Marines before his conscription age, by giving his wrong age, and had been invalided out because of foot trouble. He straightway joined the Royal Navy. His father was missing in Burma and his younger brother, aged 16, had run away to join the Merchant Navy, leaving his mother and youngest brother at home. He was the essence of boyishness; sometimes when you went to the bathroom you would find him playing the salt water hose at imaginary targets. His goodheartness was abounding, nothing was too much trouble for him such as pouring your tea, or giving a lift with a hatch, it was all the same to him. I used a glass tumbler for my tea and invariably as I lifted the fanny to pour out my tea he would jokingly admonish me and put a spoon in the tumbler to prevent its cracking. He had the habit of kneeling on the form and cupping his hands, resting his elbows on the table, and talking to you with all the verve, honesty and enthusiasm of youth. He was homesick at times and, when

54

teased, would shake his tousled head, give one of his grins and say, "No I'm not, I'm really not. But it would be alright to be in Blackpool." I certainly agreed. A crash had occurred on the flight deck about 15.40 on the 10th and a rating was killed, but that was all we knew. I had finished my tea and was smoking a cigarette when it was whispered that it was thought Bernard was the one killed. He hadn't arrived for tea, but that was not unusual; perhaps he had been detained because of accidents on the flight deck, or perhaps his natural enthusiasm for watching deck landings had detained him. We still waited for him to arrive until finally the mess president went to enquire. Apparently he had been standing near the tow motor whan an aircraft made a faulty landing and Bernard had been unable to get out of the way. I believe he had been killed instantaneously by the air screw. This news shattered the mess. A pipe was made that he would be committed to the deep at 19.00. Mr. Hudson, Bernard's Warrant Officer, was on the verge of tears. The Commander and the Paymaster Commander, and some of the officers were there on the Quarter Deck and all his messmates. His body was covered with a Union Jack. I have never seen anything so simple and solemn. Bernard was a Roman Catholic and consequently the service was read by Lieutenant Percy. The Our Father was repeated by us. The bier was lifted by his workmates and taken to the stern; the Commander placed his hands upon the bier, the body slid gently into the deep blue waters. The Mediterranean looked like unruffled silk except for the white curling wake of the ship which reached out and embraced him.

I remembered when we were in Alexandria only a few days previous to Bernard's untimely death. A few of us were leaving the ship for shore leave. It was early afternoon when we met Bernard returning. We asked him to come with us, it was so early, he could not have been ashore for an hour. We said we weren't going drinking, and he was alone and much younger than us. He hesitated then said he had bought some presents for his mother and brother and wanted to pack them safely away, and also he had some dhobi-ing to do.

At Action on the 9th some of us, when in the midst of pushing pom-pom ammunition up to the flight deck,were instructed to go and give a lift with the action there. We were glad to get out of the heat of the Servery Flat, and completely saturated, hurriedly climbed the ladders into the cold night air. The sky was ablaze with shell fire which not only illuminated the flight deck but the whole of the sea around. Every so often we could see the ships of the fleet, their guns blazing away as they glided by. The noise made by our pom-poms was terrific. This side of warfare was new to me, before we had been a few decks down with nothing to see of what was happening. During the operation there was a leak in the Admiral's Store. More work of baling out every four hours; so between humping ammunition and doing our ordinary work we were carrying buckets of water up three decks and ditching over the side. You did get a few hours sleep on the hard deck when there was a lull.

Soon news was coming through of the compliance of the Italian Fleet with the terms of surrender. Part of the Fleet sailed to Bone, part to Majorca, and other ships were sailing down the western coast of Italy. The *Valiant* and the *Warspite* left to escort them. True to German tradition the Germans attacked their late friend's fleet and a battleship thought to be the *Roma* was sunk.

On Sunday the 12th we were on our way back to Malta. We were to have passed through the Straits of Messina on the night of Saturday-Sunday but, possibly by reason of Heinkels and F.W'S keeping watch on us, we sailed round the westerly coast of Sicily. The island of Pantellaria was passed on Sunday morning and I had a good view of the Italian Malta. A small village hugged the sea shore, whilst further up the hillside the famous white houses of the island could be seen. We sailed into Valetta with part of the famous Italian Fleet.

The mainbrace was spliced on Sunday, 12th September,

1943, in celebration of the surrender of the Italian Fleet and the success of the operation of Force H. On the 17th September the Skipper spoke to us that night and told us of this operation by Force H. Apparently the uneconomic use of the navy resulted in our being withdrawn and many ships had been hit. Today I saw the *Savannah*, an American cruiser being towed. She had been hit by a rocket bomb and 16 officers and over 200 ratings had been killed. The *Uganda* had also been hit, but the damage had not been as severe as that done to the *Savannah*. Glider bombs were now being used by the Axis power.

Today the effects of Bernard Foley were sold on the flight deck. They realised £100.

The Skipper told us that Mussolini, who had been under close arrest in Sardinia, had been rescued by German paratroopers and had returned to Rome from whence he had probably gone to Northern Italy's Lake Como area.

A Canadian officer told us of the great part played by the Canadians in this war. One telling thing he said was that many people had been unemployed and of them their Prime Minister had said they would not get a 5 cent piece from him. These same men who had been called bums had hitch hiked to join up and had given their lives in Hong Kong, Dieppe and North Africa. He thought that Canada would, after the war, look after such men, and would remain British and that no disquiet would arise from the French Canadians. The Commander always made a comment upon any message given over the tannoy, a word of thanks and an expression to hear the speaker again, but on this occasion he made no comment at all.

September 18th. My birthday and Herringbone won the St. Leger. Courtesy of radio.

September 19th. With a church parade from the ship we went to St. Andrew's Presbyterian Church, Malta. The church which was built by the efforts of Dr. and Mrs Wisely, D.D. had suffered slightly from the bombardment. The morning was really warm; below us we saw the *Warspite* which had just been towed into harbour; she, too, had been hit at Salerno and was well down in the water.

Monday 20th. We left Malta in company with the *Illustrious* and a few destroyers. The buzz was very strong. Gibraltar and then U.K. Many happy faces on board today. A number of Canadian matelots came aboard; they understood we were taking them to the U.K. and they were on their way to Quebec. We passed Pantellaria and Cape Bon today.

We arrived at Gibraltar at 11.00 on the 22nd. The following day many escorts arrived and Captain P. Ruck-Keene, C.B.E. our new skipper joined today

On the 27th we left for exercises. Captain Talbot, our late Skipper, left the ship today. In a brief message he told us he was leaving for the U.K. in a Liberator and he thought we would be there soon. He was well liked. His nick-name was Nutty. Apparently he enjoyed his ration of sweets from the shop on board.

We left harbour on the 5th October at 20.00. Everyone had stocked up with green bananas, lemons, etc. bought in the anticipation of going home. The *Valiant* and *Illustrious* were with us and many destroyers. Everyone was in high spirits when the new Skipper told us that we were on our way home to that mythical isle of dreams. There was much speculation as to where we would dock, when the bomb fell. We had been recalled. Only a day or so from home and the Mediterranean was pining for us to go back. Those few words sapped the life out of us. High language never was so high. Buzzes were started again. Bananas and lemons were being eaten.

Panic for evermore. We were transferring Albacores to the *Illustrious*, she was giving Martlets and Seafires. I worked through the night bringing aircraft on lighters to our ship. The huge machines seemed to swing for evermore over the side of the ship, whilst aircraft handling parties struck them below, or pushed them about the flight deck.

The next important day was Friday. I attended the preliminary hearing of the recommendation for a commission. The Board consisted of Commander G. Thistleton-Smith, the Paymaster Commander Selwood, and the Captain's Secretary, Lieutenant H. C. Lamb. Usually you are sent to England for the hearing.

I was ushered into the Commander's cabin and told to be seated. The first question I failed to hear. Brilliant. I think the Commander should not have asked it while looking down into a sheaf of papers (my record) but should have directed it straight at me.

First question: "How did you hurt your thumb?" I replied that the bomb lift on which I was working had not been at the correct level or the accident would not have happened. Wrong diplomacy.

Next question: "What is a proximal phalanx?" Me thinking (but not speaking), proximo=next to: phalanx=body of Roman soldiers who fought in a column with shields over their heads and covering their sides. I could not make any connection. I replied that I did not know. The Captain's Secretary gurgled and waving his thumb said, I know that—your thumb.

This was Goodbye Commission.

Next: "What is your father's occupation?" "A locomotive engineer, but I do not see that his occupation matters." I knew I had blown it."Is he alive ?" "No Sir." "When did he die?" "Two years ago, sir." "I see that you are a Methodist." "Yes, sir." "Do you attend church?" "Yes, sir." "Then where is the Methodist Church in Gibraltar?" "It is Providence Chapel, it is in Prince Edward Road and the minister is the Rev. Fred. E. Brown, and he is no relation of mine." I thought they could have the lot. The Paymaster then questioned me, "Do you find any work more interesting than others?" "No, sir. As you know I recently transferred from one section to another, and asked to be transferred to the Fleet Air Arm section so as to gain an all round

59

experience and see how one section complements the other." "When did you decide on a commission?" "I didn't. Captain Woodhouse decided at the Naval School of Accountancy and recommended me as a result of the examination at the end of the course. I was pleased and made no objection." "Why do you think you would make a good officer?" "I have professional qualifications in Commerce; my position was a legal and admininstrative assistant with a large local authority. I think these fit me better to serve than as a Supply Assistant." "You do, do you? What do you do in your spare time?" "I play bridge." "Do you use the ship's library?" "Unfortunately the library consists mostly of westerns and crime. I prefer more serious reading. There are good writers of these subjects, but those in the library are of the lurid type." The Paymaster: "I like westerns." The Captain's Secretary; "I like thrillers." I thought it was Tweedle Dum and Tweedle Dee.

"Do you attend the ship's cinema, and what do you think of the films?" "I rarely attend, but I would like to see some films which are not westerns." "But most of the ship's company like westerns." "I suppose so." "Do you speak German fluently, so as to listen to News Bulletins?" "No, sir. I took it to matriculation standard but have allowed it to be neglected, hence my attempts at brushing it up." "What were your duties in civilian employment?" "I was a Committee Clerk, I convened the meetings, prepared the agenda, wrote up the minutes, acted upon the resolutions passed, liaised with the other sections, and dealt with the correspondence arising." "Can you do shorthand?" "Yes, sir, I've done some for you on the Petrol Fire Inquiry." "Oh."

This is not a verbatim record but gives an overall idea of the interview. Personally I do not think I would have made a good officer.

I was afterwards sent for and the Commander said something like this, all the time avoiding my gaze. "It is difficult in a few minutes to assess, yet I have to do it. I am not recommending your name to the Captain. There is something additional to doing a job particularly well.

Something also is required of an officer than ability to do a job. I consider you have not a wide enough outlook and hence cannot judge you. If and when you assume responsibility your commission papers will be re-opened."

I thanked him and wandered back to the mess feeling dejected. The mess were sympathetic and surprised. I think the fact that I had not applied for my leading rate to which I was entitled perhaps had something to do with it. There was a reason for my not so doing and now I will tell it, but could not at the time. An extensive racket was taking place in the Clothing Stores Accounts involving large sums of money. Sailors have a kit allowance and buy their uniforms. Some items, however, were freely renewed, for example, ratings working on aircraft wings could have their soft soled shoes renewed free of charge; certain overalls and marines boots were replaced. A member of The Master at Arms would confiscate any such items sculling around on the mess decks and in collusion with the W.O. in charge of Slops these items would be returned as unserviceable and renewable without charge to the accounts. So you had articles which could then be sold without appearing in the accounts. I did not know how this was done. I was straight from training and it was my first ship, but I knew a racket was taking place. I then refused to make out the appropriate document as I had not seen the proper returns. I was offered £5 to do this job per month, I refused, and was not asked again to prepare it. I thought no one would believe a sprog rating straight from Accountancy School. I was worried and thought the way out was to ask for a transfer to some other department and that if I were not a Leading Rate, to which I was entitled, I could plead I had no responsibility if the racket were discovered. I dropped a hint to Sub-Lieutenant Eadon when stock taking was to be held but he left the ship shortly afterwards. Perhaps I should have been stronger. I felt it so much later when I was taking the notes of a court martial of one of the people concerned. He wasn't really the chief one, the real officer had left the ship before the affair was discovered.

I was still feeling very blue during the next few days. Quite a number expressed their surprise at my having dipped. Sub. Lt. Eadon told me he was disappointed at the decision as he and others had thought me first favourite for the C.W.Stakes. Perhaps I would not have made a good officer. I was cheered a day or two later when passing through the Ward Room Flat a seaman on hands and knees scrubbing the deck stopped me. He was the other rating who was not recommended for a commission. He asked and I told him of my experiences. His were worse than mine. He was told that he was not intelligent enough. All he had was a M. Economics at Glasgow. His appearance was also exceptionally smart.

October 10th: I attended the Methodist Chapel. Afterwards I went to the library to hear a gramophone recital, Beethovan's 9th Symphony played by the Philadelphia Philharmonic Orchestra conducted by Stokowski.

October 12th. The *King George V* Dance Band entertained us on the flight deck. In the evening I saw the film "Casablanca" featuring Ingrid Bergman. Very good. The next day the skipper told us we were going to the U.K. Italy had now declared war on Germany and is accepted as co-belligerent with the United Nations. Well, well.

October 15th. Day of days, we enter the Clyde and dock at Greenock. Bert Chandler, Max Jacobs and I went ashore with the intention of phoning home. I think a million other ratings had the same idea. We managed to get a kiosk and I was most successful, I got through in two minutes but there was no reply, (completely forgiven, they were out exercising my dog.) Bert got through to Chapel-en-le-Frith in an hour. We whiled away the time eating chips out of newspapers, and in the street. And did those chips taste good! It was worth the scramble getting ashore. To do so we first of all fell in on the Forward Lift Well. Some fell in the scuppers so dark it was, and they climbed out covered in oil and water which are not supposed to mix. The lighter "Thrush" was packed, but who cared? To reach the shore you had to scramble over other lighters, never was there an obstacle race so difficult, but accepted so cheerfully. We had looked forward to setting foot on U.K. soil but no one kissed the precious earth.

October 19th. The *Queen Mary's* billet was vacated and the *Queen Elizabeth* took her place.

During these few days the Custom officals came on board. Messes mustered their rabbits—silk stockings, leather work, sandals, cosmetics, and many other exotic gifts from abroad bought on our shopping expeditions. All these items were assessed and the duty paid on the nail. I was charged 1s/8d. for two pairs of silk stockings.

The next leave at Greenock was also enjoyable, a tea of fresh fish cooked to perfection and served on decent crockery was like being at home. Afterwards Bert and I went to a dance at the Town Hall. The floor was not too good, the band very ordinary, the hall was packed and our leave was short, but it seemed enjoyable.

Sunday the 24th. The sun shone, the banks of the Clyde were green, but we went to sea and arrived at Scapa Flow on the 25th, where short shore leave was given and I went. Flotta was not interesting. To go ashore we had to go down a rope ladder from the midship pocket. All we could do was see a film at the Naval Canteen and take a short stroll along the shore path. It was U.K. so it was appreciated.

On the 27th our new Commander, D. G. Alers-Hankey arrived to take up his duties. The old Commander gave us the "gen" of the future. Most of the old crew would be drafted, that the ship would be having a re-fit, and that we would be getting leave sometime.

On the 28th we exercised and quite a few kites became unserviceable. We returned and then left for Iceland. A few weeks ago we had been working in shirts and sandals, now we were due for the frozen north. It certainly got cold, no wonder, we had passed into the Arctic Circle and docked in Eyja Fiord on the north side of the land. We were near the settlement of Akureyri but my watch did not get ashore. I was told the people were well dressed in European style. The men wore lounge suits and the ladies dresses and silk stockings. They were tall, good looking and mostly blonde. You could see the yellow walled houses with red roofs. The main street went straight up the hill. There were many smart American cars there. The fiord is exceptionally pretty. The hills are snow covered, the snow reaching three quarters of the way down. A real post card scene. It looked as if rivulets of icing had run down to the sea. Sunday was like a spring day. The sun shone, the water was a clear blue which matched the sky, the snow capped hills glistened and it was still not our watch's turn to go ashore. I wondered what the people in those lovely houses did for a living. I would have liked to have walked from Oddeyri Pier to the settlement of Akureyri. That night the Northern Lights were seen. They were like a theatre fly curtain stretching across the fiord from hill to hill—a greenish yellow bow which slowly spiralled. The weather worsened suddenly and we had difficulty in bringing back the ratings who had gone ashore so wild was the water. It was difficult to walk on the flight deck, you leaned into the strong wind, yet it was exhilarating. We put extra clothing on our hammocks, so cold it was.

We sailed at 09.00 on the 2nd November. The sun was just rising—its red light streaked the sky and suffused the snow-covered hills with orange, red and purple. At 12.30 we nosed out into the ocean, the sun well up, and at the end of the fiord the snow sparkled on the peaks. We were informed that night we were to protect a Russian Convoy, probably the last one of the year.

It was bitterly cold and the ship plunged and rolled to my discomfort which stopped short of seasickness. The convoy had been delayed for 24 hours by reason of the bad weather and this kept us out longer than had been anticipated. We had to guard the convoy should the German dive bombers spot the convoy from their bases in Northern Norway. A signal from A2 announced that the convoy should have reached the cover of Jan Mayer Island. We then thought we would then be going to dock for the refit but *Formidable* kept its reputation. Another flap had arisen. The Yankee carrier, *Ranger*, ourselves and other ships were to take part in an attack on German units, probably the *Tirpitz*, *Gneisenau*, etc. The operation was to be short. Good news: the operation was off because of treacherous weather. I didn't mind that although I had a sneaking conceit for further action against such a foe as the German, but I was glad it was off.

We sailed from Scapa on the 12th and arrived at Greenock on the 13th. We now commenced de-storing. What a job. De-ammunitioning, de-storing, de-everything. Rush and bustle in orderly disorder. Squadrons were getting ready to fly off. Stores were packed feverishly; 4.5. pom-poms, bombs and miscellaneous shells were swinging along conveyors; cases were hoisted everywhere; and lighters alongside received sufficient to sink them. Music while you work. Records played continuously throughout the day as we went to it. The Commander gave four-hourly bulletins of the progress and praised it. Time and Motion study.

During the Arctic cover I had a reporting job to do, in addition to my other work, for the Commander. A gun in Martlet 282 had fired accidentally in the hangar injuring three ratings and a full inquiry was held. This ran to about 8,000 words. The ship was rolling and rocking. At times my hand wavered in mid air and crashed down on the shorthand pad. Outlines Pitman had never designed! But worse was to follow. Typing! The machine slid past me by a yard on either side at each roll of the ship. It was with a contortionist's skill I hit the keys at times. I decided on another office where I could place the typewriter at right angles from stem to stern, so that it moved towards me. The result was better. I remembered the remark at my appearance before the commissioning board—assuming responsibility. Here I was doing what the C.P.O. Writer should have done and received extra pay for it, yet did not do it. I got 3d. extra.

Finally the day came for the squadrons to leave and I lost my particular oppoes: Bob Coggins, Spike Mullins and Jack Cruikshank. We couldn't always get ashore together, we were in different watches. I learned later that Spike was drowned at sea.

We left harbour and Greenock. For over an hour we stood at attention in the biting cold foggy atmosphere without overcoats. The Marine Band played. A few hours later we went through the same routine of falling in for entering Belfast Lough. It was foggy so no one saw anything. The band played "Here we are again".

The next few days were again hectic. We had to de-store the remainder and to make matters worse the power on the lifts and cranes was cut-off. Fuel economy meant man-handling cases and man wastage. Starting work on the jetty in darkness with hands which soon became numbed was far from pleasant. Stand-easy to thaw your fingers round a mug of tea was welcome. Cases which were too heavy to lift were pitched down the narrow gangways, many times breaking and vomiting their contents over the jetty. The work parties were chokker and cursing was *de rigeur*. We stole cases from the dump to pack stores and kept an eye for the dockyard officals who were far from pleased with the rough treatment and the breaking of the gangway steps.

We received all night leave in Belfast, that does not mean every night, it depended on which watch you were in, but it was some compensation as the ship, except for the dock maties working aboard, appeared deserted, and was bitterly cold.

Sunday in Belfast was quiet. The YMCA Hall would have an afternoon congregation of thousands at its service. At night one or two clubs were open. I went to an informal concert at the Overseas Club. Very select, but homely.

66

Anyone who could sing, recite, or play the piano did so. I was very happy to sit in a comfortable easy chair and talk to a charming Swiss girl next to me. During the week I went dancing at Albert White's and visited the Repertory Theatre.

Then the great day of leave had arrived at last, from the 27th November to the 28th December, 1943. We packed the night before and fell in in the hangar at 12.30 the next day. Those going on leave and draft had fallen in an hour before. Their kit and hammocks had been stowed in the hangar early in the morning in dumps according to their port divisions and coloured accordingly. Now we waited for snap searchings by custom officals for contraband and a few were caught out.

This meant stoppage of leave, possibility of de-rating, or cells.

At the end of a couple of hours the *Royal Daffodil* drew alongside, a gangway was thrown across from the midship pocket. The next process of loading kit and hammocks commenced. Chairs were made by ratings on draft and slowly, because of the tortuous way of getting on the *Royal Daffodil*, the baggage was finally loaded. At last the R.D. was under weigh. We watched the *Formidable* as we pulled away. There were many unmentionable comments made to officers waving us off. I could see the weak smile of the padre and his fluttering hand wave. I could hear the loud guffaw of the Commander.

Peter Hibbert, Bill Nicholas, Alf Leeming, Max Jacobs and I found wooden berths in the lowest deck and lay low. Soon Stranraer was reached and the voice of our Navigator loomed through the ship. Everyone must give a lift with getting the baggage off or the trains would not wait for us. The five lay low. We'd carry our own baggage, but not the officers', P.Os and C.P.Os luggage, we'd had enough of humping for a long time.

The Scots' party went off by buses, The London and Midlands and East Coast parties followed next. Finally those for the Crewe train left. I travelled with Fred Cadby from our mess and George Micklewright from New Moston. George and I broke the journey at Carlisle and had a snack at the Queens Canteen outside the station.

We caught the 00.55 connection and arrived at Exchange Station, Manchester about 07.45. It was raining . Slowly we made our way to Stevenson Square and boarded a New Moston bus. I arrived home at 08.30 on Sunday morning, 28th November, 1943. During this leave I managed to book two seats at the Palace Theatre, Manchester, for me and my youngest brother, Harry. He was on leave from the Army. The show was Irving Berlin's "This is the Army." Wonderful tunes, lively dancing. Marvellous. Hubert, my eldest brother also came on leave from the RAF so you can imagine the ribbing we gave each other. My sister, Nell, did fire watching at work and Home Guard duties. A suggestion was made that my mother, a widow and well turned sixty, should perhaps do war work. There were young women without children and not ill themselves whose husbands weren't in the forces who were not doing anything at all. My comments were unprintable.

1944

Thursday, 17th February, 1944 I caught the 09.30 train Victoria Station. In the same coach were a Scots guardsman from Handforth and a few Polish soldiers. We were soon talking. The guardsman had been been recalled and was expecting embarking for Algiers. Discussion followed and other places such as Trondheim and Dunkirk were mentioned. Not all conversation was on the war.

The day was sunny and the countryside was pleasant as it rushed past our window. All along the route was evidence of the ploughing orders—brown earth upturned and sweet. Westmorland and Cumberland, counties of sweeping hills and clear streams, scattered farmhouses and grazing sheep. England.

At Carlisle a crowd of youngsters, looking as if they had not long left school, disembarked. They were poorly clad, some with small cases, good and otherwise; some with coats, many without; and a few in Home Guard uniform. This was obviously a new intake at Carlisle. Then I remembered the anxious faces of relatives who had seen them off on the platform at Manchester.

Soon we were in Scotland and Lockerbie (memory of a stranded stoker at Carlisle trying to reach Lockerbie) and Symington were passed. I alighted at Carstairs and caught the Edinburgh train on the adjoining platform.

The Border counties were delightful. The hayricks here are not rectangular shaped like the English ricks, but are circular and built on a platform with a conical roof. We arrived at Princess Street Station, Edinburgh, and joined up with a Fleet Air Arm mechanic, who was already four hours adrift from his ship at Rosyth. We took the street car to Waverley Station and caught immediately a connection to Inverkeithing. I crossed over the the Forth Bridge for the second time. From here I caught the Dunfermline bus to

Rosyth Cross and then changed to the Rosyth Dockyard Bus. The dockyard was busy; the *Indefatigable* was in, smart in her ultramarine paint.

I went aboard the *Cochrane* and reported and left for something to eat at Inverkeithing. As it was now about 19.30 it wasn't worth going to Edinburgh so I returned to Rosyth and booked a bed at the British Sailors' Society. This was excellently appointed and I slept in a cubicle, No. 69. I was awakened at 06.30 and made my way down in the darkness to the dockyard and the *Cochrane*. Many dockies were leaving work after a night shift.

The fire fighting parties were now dribbling in, although many were adrift when it was time to start. The lectures were given by a W.O., who was far from eloquent. Practical work was done in the afternoon under the supervision of a Chief Stoker who was well spoken and efficient. I managed to put the fire out without difficulty. One unfortunate incident occurred.A very young rating did not show much aptitude in handling the apparatus. The Chief very patiently tried to help him overcome his disability by taking him in the pitch dark and smoke filled shed to put the fire out. The effort was not a success as the Chief emerged after an age a little shaken. Firefighting over we caught the lorry to Inverkeithing and entrained for Princess Street to catch the 17.45 to Carlisle. We went by Galashiels and Hawick. I dined at the Queens Club at Carlisle before going to see my youngest brother who was in the Loyals and stationed at the Crown and Mitre Hotel.

Harry had to report at the Castle so I took a stroll round Carlisle. I slept that night on a camp bed and the following morning breakfasted excellently on army food. The Army Catering Corps were doing a fantastic job; the rissole was superb, the bacon and beans were the best I had tasted for some time. I was impressed by Carlisle especially the sandstone Law Courts and the fine entrance they made to English Street. The block of adjoining shops erected in sandstone harmonised with the Law Courts. Many people were shopping and they looked prosperous. George the cook, whom I had met before, came to the rescue with a good dinner (a real chop) baked potatoes and swedes, followed by prunes and custard. A CCC mealtime conversation is similar to navy topics. I fell for "Bluebells I gather". On Saturday I strolled round the park which adjoins the banks of the River Eden, a salmon river. After a snack at the John Peel Club we went to dine at the Citadel, a state operated cafe. This was a delightful restaurant with good service and excellent cuisine. I went to Chisams Hotel in Botchergate to get ready for the night's entertainment, afterwards picking up Harry at his quarters. Mac and Alf joined us as we caught the bus to St. Margaret Mary's. Prior to this we had a few drinks at a nearby hotel, where Jock and Smudgy joined us. Being the only naval rating there I was inundated with questions on navy life. There was a good mood there and I enjoyed myself.

After breakfast I took my luggage to the station and found the first boat train was at 00.15. I joined Harry again and had a chat with his Major, a delightful gentleman. Once again George helped out with dinner; again it was first class. During the afternoon I slept, then had tea at the CWL and afterwards went with Mac and Alf to see "The Eagle Has Wings" at the Lonsdale; Ann Sheridan and George Meredith were the stars. Afterwards we all went to the John Peel Hut where the Border Regiment Dance Band were playing, "D'ye ken John Peel". We had tea at the Crown and Mitre.

Harry saw me off on the train. A few of *Formidable's* crew were arriving and we chatted over what we had been up to. One Yorkshire lad, with a few hours to spare had wandered in search of a pub, and had to his disgust accepted an offer of a meal and found himself at a Mission Hall. His description of the elderly ladies there, the hymns he sang, and the ecstatic delight over one saved, was exceptionally funny. Jamieson joined us, the train was late and crowded. I stood in the corridor, there were no vacant seats. Stranraer was reached about 05.00 and I went aboard and found a form to lie on. We entered Larne about 11.30. The sea

71

danced in the sunlight. There was the usual delay in disembarking, finally I got off, found a seat on the train to Belfast. Larne to Belfast is not interesting by rail. We passed through Whitehead and Carrickfergus. As is usual industry in the form of the British Portland Cement Co. had turned the area derelict. The tall cranes which dominate Belfast's skyline came into view. I travelled with Cockayne down to the ship first having dined at the Imperial. The *Formidable* was still in dry dock. Conditions were still appalling. The ship was torn to pieces, gaping holes in the ship's sides, drilling machines made you deaf, welders showering sparks and blinding you with vivid flashes.

We found that the routine had been altered and meals were now served in Harland and Wolff's Canteen. This system was good and the cooking had improved. A large picture of the ship at Gibraltar hung over the serving counters. I slung early in order to catch up with sleep, but drilling machines just above my head were going continuously until breakfast time. The ship was having a complete overhaul: new water-tight compartments similar to those on German ships. More armament was being fitted and many more improvements to increase the efficiency of the ship and make it more safe. When you slung your hammock you could see through the gaping sides where plates had been removed. There was no protection from wind and rain which whistled through, sometimes carrying specks of snow. Sometimes sparks from the welders cutting the deck above showered into your hammock and then you beat a hasty retreat and found another slinging space. Not amusing when the cold wind was whistling through your legs and you completely in the nuddy. We would be at work early on the dockside and in the dark, sometimes in snow, yet I never had a cold and in your hammock you were completely warm.

I was now working in Naval Stores and in charge of Radar and W/T Stores and other stores which were assigned to me on the 22nd February, 1944.

A small draft arrived on Wednesday, three S.A's coming to our mess. At night Harland and Wolff's employees gave us a concert in the canteen. It was really good. The following night I went with Alf to see James Bridie's play, Mr. Bolfry, at the Group Theatre in Bedford Street. The action of the play is set in the Manse of a Free Church in the Highlands of Scotland and deals with Calvinistic doctrine. It was excellently produced and brilliantly acted. The Group Theatre is small, it corresponds with the Abbey Theatre in Dublin. Much later, and as a complete change, I went to the Empire where "Come to the Show", a variety show in its third year, was showing. There was a change of programme every week, the company were resident. I could not understand why it lasted so long, yet I must confess that I always enjoyed myself when I went there.

The weather changed again on Saturday, turning bitterly cold, snow was now driving in horizontal streaks. The hills surrounding Belfast were capped with snow. I stayed on board. An amusing incident in the mess. Don Beadle, a newly arrived F.A.A. Supply Assistant said that at the commencement of the war he was an evacuee. At that time I was up to the eyes in work on evacuation schemes. Nothing exciting this week. Jimmy O'Dea's Show, "This is the Blarney" was most amusing especially his gibes at Fenian songs.

The following Saturday Alf and I decided to go to Bangor. We caught the 13.50 train from County Down Station (fare 1s/3d. for servicemen). A clergyman leaned out of a carriage window and asked us if he were on the right train to Craigavon. I knew this uniform would have us carrying suit cases. The journey to Bangor took about 1½ hours and was interesting. There was the aerodrome at Sydenham and Hollywood. Further pleasant vistas of woodlands appear at Craigavon. The line in places hugs the shore of Belfast Lough down the centre of which are anchored the buoys indicating the channel. Perhaps the day was not too good for visiting, it was cold and squally. I was not impressed as we walked down the main street to the front.

A fine view of the sea dancing with white horses and with a frigate and a destroyer riding gracefully at anchor was framed in between the sides of the street. We turned right at the bottom of Main Street and continued along the shore road. The boarding houses were not out of the ordinary, the beach was rocky with a few small scaly patches. Over the rise we came to the municipal greens and obtained views of Ballyholme Bay. There are better class houses here and the Flamingo Ballroom and Caponi's Cafe which add to the appearance. We returned to the old part of Bangor by way of High Street and after a snack made for the Tonic Picture House, one of the super-de-luxe theatres, which together with the Savoy are the best buildings. "Reveille with Beverly" was the programme being shown featuring Ann Miller, Bob Crosby's, Tommy d'Orsay's, Duke Ellington's and Cab Calloway's bands, and with Frank Sinatra and the Mills Brothers.

On Tuesday was announced the loss of the light cruiser *Penelope* which had been with us during the last commission. I recalled that I nearly said yes to an exchange of places with an S.A. aboard *Penelope*, who was not too happy. The *Penelope* had seen a lot of action: Malta, Pantellaria, Lampadusa and for obvious reasons had earned the soubriquet HMS *Pepper Pot*.

On Monday I went ashore with Jim Slater, a writer from Oldham who had just joined us. He was looking for a laundry and I offered to show him the place where I left my soiled clothes, the ship being impossible for dhobi-ing. We had tea at the Imperial and afterwards went book browsing near Smithfield Market. I bought Kenneth Robert's Rabble in Arms, J.S. Mills' On Liberty and the Subjection of Women. I had not enough funds or I would have purchased Ibanez' The Mob, and Delafield's Diary of a Provincial Lady, and a book of Conrad's short stories. In passing much later on I was asked had I anything to read and I said help yourself from my locker. He took out Mills' book On Liberty. In a short time he came back with it complaining

74

that he thought it was a story of a matelot on shore leave!

We whiled away half an hour at the Christian Science's Rooms which were very comfortable, so much that we nearly stayed the whole evening. We forced ourselves out of the comfortable armchairs and away from the peat fire and dashed round to the Empire. The usual company was there and everyone joined in singing lustily the Irish song "Moonshine", and the lastest comedy hit "Pistol Packing Mamma". Later in the week Alf and I had a quiet run to the Astoria where two very ordinary films were being shown. Sometime later we had the advantage of a weekend leave and I suggested we go to Portrush. To provide for the expense we stayed on board for a whole week.

Saturday came and Alan Hislam decided to join us. Inspection of Liberty Men was a complete bind. The Duty Officer was very late in arriving to inspect us, and when he did arrive he gave each one the closest personal inspection. Men in white caps were picked up and one without the stiffener in his cap. He paused before every one of us and we inwardly cursed. Our train was at 14.00 at York Street and 13.30 had already gone. Finally we got away and hared to York Street with a couple of minutes to spare.

Our travelling companions in the train were a RAF officer and a Yankee soldier. After a while we thawed and soon were on friendly terms with the American. He came from North Dakota and my comments about the sparsely populated countryside through which we were passing brought him into the conversation. He talked of Service Clubs and American Army rations in the way of razor blades, chocolate, gum, cookies etc. One confection he mentioned was mouth watering. It was called Babe Ruth Chocolate Bars, although he informed us the Yanks now only got English austerity chocolate.

I would like to have gone by the coast road but war prevented this. I was surprised by the smallness of the towns through which we passed, places well known that I thought must be large. Antrim looked like a village. We did not see views of Lough Neagh. Coleraine, Ballymoney and

Ballymena were quite small. We reached Portrush about 16.10. The station is half timbered, and close by were the American Red Cross establishments, games rooms, lounges, etc. We had been informed of an address where we could be welcomed. Micky McCausland a native of Bushmills near Portrush and of our ship's company said that as soon as we mentioned his name we would be offered accommodation. We asked directions of this place from passers by but no one seemed to know where it was. At last we came to what most certainly it was. We knocked at the door and enquired if Micky McCausland was known to them. A look of complete denial came over the face of the girl. Perhaps it was some other place. We bent our frames into the driving rain. It was now turned 6 p.m. and still no digs. Hunger assailed us so we dined and discussed what to do. We had seen Castle Erin the C.E. Holiday Home poster near the station. We went back there but the Home was on a cliff edge when we finally found it. When we reached the door, we read a notice "Ministry of Education". Back to Main Street. Who was it had suggested Portrush were the accusing glances. We stopped a policeman, the only person we had seen in this driving rain, and asked him if he could recommend a place for us to stay. He took us to the Seymour Hotel, Bath Terrace, owned by Mrs. Marshall who fixed us up. We deposited our belongings and left for amusement after trying to spruce ourselves. The other two went to the Cinema, I went dancing at the Palladium. This had a good spring floor and the crowd was good. The British Services were represented by four Wrens, two RAF one South Lancashire Fusilier and me. The rest were American soldiers and sailors. I enjoyed the evening. One of the Wrens who came from Edinburgh was a good dancer English style, and so were the others. They had to leave early to go on "sparking duties". I stayed to the end. An American had joined our group and we left together, but the cold wet wind had sent scurrying home the dancers so it was no use our feeling randy. We would have had no success in attracting any one of them on a night like that.

I returned to the Seymour. Alf and Alan were asleep. I retired to my room, first opening the curtains so I could see the sea when morning came. Months of early awakening had seeped into my system. I woke at 6 a.m. but stayed in bed until 9 a.m. No getting out of a hammock and lashing up and stowing. The view from the window was superb. Breakers were breaking and tumbling all along and dashing themselves over the Skerries a low reef of rocks stretching across the bay and lending a pleasing aspect to the panorama. We breakfasted on bacon and egg, wheatmeal bread and cups of tea with plenty of sugar. After breakfast we took a stroll along the beach. It was pleasant listening to the roar of the breakers and being sprayed with saltwater.

A dog dashed out of the scrub grass and tagged on to us. It brought back a stone we had been throwing and laid it down at our feet. Then he would lie down and look expectantly at us. We enjoyed the fun but had a dickens of a job to get rid of him. As we had decided to visit the Giant's Causeway, and that was the purpose of visiting Portrush, we took an early meal at the Seymour. What a dinner! Soup, main course consisting of roast (more meat on my plate than a week's rations) a tureen of jacket potatoes, cabbage, finishing off with creamed rice and prunes and coffee.

We boarded the tram near the railway station; the tram consisted of three coaches, one enclosed the other two were open toast racks with canvas sides should the weather prove inclement. The track ran along the coast and splendid views were obtained of the bay. Small coves where seagulls were resting on the ledges were innumerable. On one headland the ruins of Dunluce Castle added a romantic touch to the picture. The castle was built about 1400 years ago and was rebuilt in the 16th Century. The walls are greenish brown and blend with the surrounding rocks. We reached the Causeway and paid 6d. to enter. Of course there had to be a wishing well. The rock formation was quite regular, hexagon shaped stones piled one above the other forming pillars which fitted together like a jigsaw puzzle. A large area is covered by this formation but most of it cannot be seen. We walked along the rock side at our risk, so the notice board told us. The pathway rose and fell with the rock strata from which it had been hacked. The various strata were clearly discernable, on top was the lava formation, next the red stone, and below a greenish grey rock.

At one point the rocks were not touching and the effect was of Giant Organ Pipes. A vast amphitheatre was explored.

Many American soldiers were visiting the Causeway and most of them had very expensive cameras. They appeared to be able to get films without difficulty.

We arrived back at Portrush about 18.00 and had an excellent tea. Three American sailors were also dining at the Seymour, at our table. We spoke to them but they appeared embarrassed. Unless they were talking to each other they appeared uneasy. They have a different way of eating from us. They cut up the meat first, then take the fork in the right hand and pick up the pieces.

We caught the 19.30 train back to Belfast. The journey was uneventful as far as Antrim, although an American's comments upon the weather in California drew from Alf his experiences in Iceland and the Mediterranean, and from Alan a pungent aside about Chewme, on the China Station. I said the journey was uneventful, but at Antrim a crowd of camp followers besieged the compartment. Two of them were about sixteen years of age saying farewell to Negro troops. During the conversation which passed between them after the train left Antrim was the remark that she had 'gone for five shillings'. Whether she had paid the train fare out of it I don't know.

On returning to the ship we discovered the house that Micky McCausland had recommended to us was the one we went to. Such is the Irish Blarney.

During the next week Alf, Johnny, Ginger and I visited the Group Theatre to see 'Jupiter Laughs' by A.J. Cronin. It was very well acted and really enjoyable.

On Thursday night I went ashore at the invitation of

McCullough to a Caleidhea. I joined him at a house in Grand Parade, Bloomfield and afterwards we called for Betty Girvan who lived at a house called Meiringen in the same road. This name brought back good and happy memories of a holiday spent in Switzerland before the war, of Rosenlauie and over the top to Grindelwald passing the Uber and Unter Gletscher. Mrs. Girvan was a homely lady and gave me a standing invitation to visit whenever I liked.

The Caleidhea, (pronounce caley) was great fun, all Irish dancing. I was dragged to the floor for the first gig, a Ringemore. I cannot describe these set dances but the main step is the gig-step, a tap with the right foot in front of the left, then two taps behind; afterwards you reverse. Another important step carries you sideways, one foot passing behind the other. In whirling round you grasp your partner's right hand in yours, shoulder high, and with the left hand grasp her right elbow. For the life of me what she does with her left hand I don't know, except she holds on to you with it. I think that's correct. If it isn't don't fall on the floor. The Ringemore was followed by the Walls of Limerick and again I was on my feet or someone else's. I sat out an eight hand reel and a sixteen hand reel as these were far too complicated to understand. Jackets were now peeled and perspiration was staining shirts. It was surprising how easily feet flashed round the slippery floor. The going was furious. The Haymakers Gig, and High Pole Cat were hectic. I took part in the more sedate Dashing White Sergeant, which would put many a jitterbug in the cissy category. I believe I got up for the Haymakers Gig and certainly did for the Siege of Venice and the Siege of Carrick. The band consisted of an accordion, drums and, of course, a fiddle.

St. Patrick's Day, and I was on duty. How I wished I was at a gig. On Saturday I saw a football match, Linfield v Distillery at Windsor Ground. The attraction for me was that Stan Pearson, a Manchester United player and now in the army was guesting in this match. In the evening I had a couple of hours to spare before going to a dance. I decided to visit the Falls Road an area out of bounds. First of all I played for safety and went by bus which goes along the Falls and alighted at Andersonstown. The Falls is a notorious I.R.A. area where trouble boils up and has to be cordoned off at times when there is restlessness. Armoured cars sometimes go to quell the trouble. It is a poor quarter similar to others in the protestant areas. It is dirty, untidy but it has a fascination of its owm. This is the land of the Kellys, Flannigans and Muldoons; the Liams, Cormacs and Seans. Dirty dimly lit shops huddle together with squat mean houses in between. Bars are busy and children throng their doors. It was most interesting and I wished I could have found a dance in progress. Perhaps I was fortunate that I did not do so as I learned afterwards that one of our patrols had been beaten up the previous week in this district.

On Sunday I planned an afternoon to go to Grey Abbey. We passed the Houses of Parliament at Stormont and afterwards reached Newtonards with its tall stone Town Hall.

It was a delightful Spring day, primulas, auriculas, primroses and white rock grew in profusion in the gardens. The lawns were even now cut well and trimmed. Gorse blazed in large clumps on the hillside and flowering cherry was in bloom. We walked to the end of the village and leaned on the wall and enjoyed the view of Strangford Lough. The Mountains of Mourne, blue and shadowy, broke the sky line and swept down to the sea.

Grey Abbey is a small clean village; most of its houses are white washed single storeyed buildings. Lying off the village street are the ruins of a Cistercian Monastery which we could not resist visiting. The roof is missing but the walls are in a good state of preservation. It was built in the 11th Century and possesses a lovely English doorway. It is in the possession of the Montgomery family but not related to General Monty. A few magnificent yew trees line the main walk.

We retraced our steps to Newtonards, seven miles away.

The road was alongside the lough, in parts quite close to the shore. Vast stretches of flats lay uncovered by the sea, otherwise Strangford would have been quite pretty. About two hours walking brought us to Newtonards; the tower on the hillside, overlooking the town, was visible long before we reached the town.

The following week was ordinary. Storing ship was in full swing and my most pleasant day was taking a working party to Pollard Dock West on a lorry to collect stores. The craze at the moment is to whistle the sweet young things on a high and low note, so the overall clad matelots greeted the colleens in this manner on our way to the dock.

I went with Alf to the Ambassadors at Cregagh to see "Hitler's Children" and with Jack Baron to the Classic to see "Sweet Rosie O'Grady". With the watch keeping system now in operation it happens that your leave does not correspond with those you usually go ashore with.

The next few weeks are going to be lumped together because there was blessed leave at home and blessed work day and night aboard. Leave at home would carry me over Easter and I considered myself very fortunate to be home during that period when friends would also be on holiday. I would also be missing the constant hammering and drilling which was still overhead and around.

It was pouring down in Belfast and to make matters worse the transport arrangements were non-exsistent. We lined up on the jetty, clutching our parcels and respirators, and in due time emerged on to Queens Road. I decided to walk the dreary stretch to Castle Junction when a lorry stopped and picked me up. I travelled in the cab and a dozen or so bedraggled matelots then clambered on the back.

The journey home was uneventful. 22.30 from Stranraer, the London train, change at Wigan and Exchange, caught the 06.00 train for Clayton Bridge and arrived home at 06.30. Breakfast, delicious. Bed, heavenly.

I returned on the 13th April this time getting the 14.40 from Exchange and changed at Hellifield which is high on the moors. It was cold and bleak exposed to all the winds.

I arrived at Carlisle at 19.00 and after a meal with Harry went to H.M. Theatre and suffered an extremly poor show.

Once more I endured travelling on a troop luxury rail car—stand all the way either on your feet or on someone else's. It was comfort indeed to emerge at Stranraer at 04.00 and go through the rigorous customs search. Newspapers and similar items were confiscated, the ban on Ireland was in being, the Second Front could not be far off. I got back on board about 14.30 on the 14th April after dining at the Orpheus Cafe.

Bed and work was the routine during the next few weeks and very little bed. Leave was drastically cut, and even watch ashore was at the earliest 19.00 which left little time to do anything. Storing, striking down, working parties, cranes, humping, the whole labourious round of storing ship kept you busy from early morn till late at night, and your meal periods were cut. The ship was becoming unhappy, crime (naval) was on the increase, and punishment was severe. Warrants were increasing and the cells at Preston and Caroline must have been reserved exclusively for *Formidable's* ratings. Snooping was de rigeur and your life was not your own. The watch-word was "This is the hourly warrant and so-and-so reading it" or the pipe "Men under punishment stay on your mess decks, the other two ratings muster on the gangway."

Despite all this I was enjoying life and was considerably cheered when at last I was able go to the Group Theatre to see "The Old Broom."

On returning I saw painted on the bows of the ship in large letters ALTMARK II.

On the 20th April I went to the Empire with a number from the mess to attend the thousandth performance of "Come to the Show." I still cannot understand why it has run so long. I enjoyed the Irish ballads and the dancing. This night we were on the back row. Many bottles of liquor were being consumed in the bar. After the show we careered round Belfast and finished up at the Mayfair dancing. On the 22nd I attended the Irish Cup Final at the Windsor Grounds. Celtic 3 Linfield 1. It wasn't too good a game and there was little enthusiasm from the crowd.

On Sundays when not on duty I attended the Methodist Church on Donegal Square. It is a lovely church, cream painted walls and a beautiful mahogany rostrum. Many of the pews have brass plates in memory of some person or family who left the church some years ago and settled in Canada or America. Names of cities like New York, Pittsburgh, Philadelphia, speak of the Irish emigrants. On the 30th April when Steve and I attended the minister, Rev. Holland, invited us to supper at his house. He took us in his car and another, a Tel. from another ship, to Chlorine Gardens. What a night we had. We sat in easy chairs before an open fire and were treated as ordinary human beings. The two children, Moira Patricia aged 2½ years, and Terence, 8 months, were brought from their beds for our delight.

On Friday 5th May I went to the Floral Hall which is a dance hall situated at Glengormley in the Belle Vue Parklands. The floors is circular and the French windows at this time of year were left open revealing a panorama of the slopes of Cave Hill and the long stretch of Belfast Lough. I met Arthur Holt from Newton Heath who was in the army, and Betty McManus of Lisbon Street, Ballymacarett.

Betty is about 5'6" in height, brunette, brown eyes, and has a trim figure. She has, in Max's words, a delicious smile. We danced and afterwards I took her part of the way home, apparently the English were not too popular in that quarter. She worked in a clothing factory as a machinist, and the Short Strand where she lived was second only to the Falls Road. She had three brothers and attended St. Mathew's R. C. Church. I arranged to meet her again. She gave me her views on the religious controversy in Northern Ireland, but did not seem to be bitter.

During this period the Belfast Choral Society gave the

83

Gilbert and Sullivan Operas, the Mikado, and the Gondoliers. I saw the former and enjoyed it.

I saw Betty a number of times, dancing at the Floral Hall, and also at the Navy Club where the *Formidable* held a dance, and escorting her to the Group Theatre. We saw "Friends and Relations."

An amusing incident for us, but not for the person concerned, happened on the 7th May. The Leading Cook of the next mess to ours was in our mess and said in a loud voice, "If the fucking Navigator comes in now, I'll fuck him." The Navigator was standing behind him, they come upon you suddenly and silently, and took him to the Quarter Deck. I don't think the act of sodomy was performed, however!

A C.P.O. who had been at large in Belfast for a fortnight was apprehended on the 20th May. More later. During the next few days I attended the Inquiry into the charges against him, as shorthand writer. He was eventually dipped to a Leading Rate and so ended an interesting episode in Naval Accountancy. The chief culprit had escaped, he was no longer on the ship, having been drafted months ago.

Wednesday the 24th May, was the date fixed for the Writer and Supply Assistants' Outing, or for those who would not be on watch. We got permission to leave on the first boat. As usual we were too busy and couldn't go, and so went much later. Alf, Jimmy, Steve, Fred, George, Charlie and I stepped ashore and first of all we went to the barbers. We had not been ashore early for weeks owing to pressure and the shops were then closed when we did get leave. We all had the appearance of musicians. Don't play Hearts and Flowers yet. Having become respectable we sauntered to the King's Bar, near the Heysham Quay, and had enough to last the evening. The front row of the theatre had been reserved previously for us. We joined lustily in all the songs, emptied illimitable bottles of beer, and tried to put the dancers out of step. When MacNamara's Band was struck up we grouped round the coductor and Megarry lead us in discordant harmony. The balconies stood on tip toe, and cheered. After the show we raced through the streets and finished at a cafe.

Three more warrants were read. I should have met Betty tonight but had to work and missed my leave.

On Saturday the 27th we had a good view of the Swedish Hospital Ship, *Gripsholm*, steaming up to Pollock dock. She was bringing back a number of repatriated prisoners of war. She was white, had yellow funnels, and had painted on her bows in large black letters, DIPLOMAT, GRIPSHOLM, SVERIDGE. The Swedish flag was painted on her superstructure.

I was nearly done out of a make and mend, the first for many weeks but the W.O. ruled that duty watch were the ones to miss it.

I saw the farce Good Men Sleep Alone, at the Opera House on the 31st. Not bad.

Sunday the 4th June. Cold and wet. Steve and I attended the Sunday School Anniversary at the Methodist Church. The difficult pieces sung by the children were delightful to hear.

8th June. Admiral Bevan came on board and lower decks were cleared. I was on duty so did not hear the Admiral speak. Afterwards I was told that there was not true naval discipline when the Admiral spoke, but a fair amount of laughter and comments. A Leading Rate and an Able-seaman were put on charges. As usual I picked up extra work as shorthand writer.

One of the most pleasant places I visited in Belfast was the May Street Presbyterian Church Canteen, run jointly with the Methodist Church. Every Sunday night if we were ashore we went to what we nick-named the Church Door Canteen. It was situated under the church. It opened after evening service. Possibly two hundred service men and women attended. The hall was low ceilinged. Tables were attractively laid out and piled up with home-made cakes, pancakes, soda bread, sandwiches, meat pies, etc. all supplied by the congregations and gratis to the Forces. Dr. Blue, the minister of May Street, a tall and white haired patriarchal figure, invariably came in and welcomed us. Quite a few of the lads from *Formidable* were there, mostly the Radar and W/T. After supper we sang hymns, or listened to artists, all of whom were good. The M.C. was a comedian. If he thought someone was not singing he would put the spot light on them and make them sing a verse alone. Favourite hymns would be requested, but as you had to sing a verse alone, I never made a request. Why empty the hall on the first note? Favourite hymns were Guide me O Thou great Jehovah, to the tune Cwm Rhondda: By cool Siloam's shady rill, to Belmont; and Heavenly Saviour pilot me (a new one on me). An American Servicewoman usually sat with us. She was in the Red Cross and was probably about 35. She oozed charm and graciousness. She had to sing one verse and although she did not have a good singing voice we demanded a second verse from her, she was so good looking and well worth seeing. A soldier from Failsworth always joined our group.

On the 9th June we left harbour. I should have been meeting Betty. You never know when you are leaving but I managed to slip a note to her as one of our writers was going ashore to purchase essential material which might run out during our stay at sea. I did not get a reply and so ended our friendship.

I suppose it must be an interesting sight to see a ship leaving the dock with the crew lining the flight deck and luckily the weather was good. Workmen found vantage points on the ships under repair, on the stocks , and other places, to see us leave. A gun site's crew hurried down to the lough edge to watch us go. I could see the green dome of the City Hall and the thin tower of the Albert Clock. Good-bye Belfast—I've had a smashing time with you.

Before I leave Belfast I should mention other places which I appreciated. When we had money in our pockets at the beginning of the month we would book a bed at the Union

Club for 2s/6d. It was exceptionally well appointed with linen sheets on the beds and an appetising breakfast. A fortnight later when we had Saturday leave, or during the week if we had night leave and little money in our pockets we would book accommodation at the Wellington Hall. Here you slept on the floor with a blanket to cover you. You tied your boots round your wrist in case someone flogged them whilst you were asleep. An elderly gentleman chalked on the floor at your feet the time you required for a shake, usually 6 am. It was a wonderful service and greatly appreciated.

We had now left Belfast and the Captain spoke to us. We were going on trials. He had tried to get us leave but that had not been possible especially as the invasion of Europe had begun. Conditions, he said, had been and were always none too good alongside a dock wall and now we had left he wanted to make a fresh start. Consequently, all men under punishment, except men in cells, would be cancelled. He expected we might be away for two years but it must always be remembered that a carrier was not attached to any Fleet. Furthermore, he promised always to let us know what was happening, where we were going, etc. if it were possible to do so. He would never mislead us, overstate or understate events.

Action Stations were exercised on the 9th. Mine was now in the First Aid Party. The next two weeks we exercised. We saw many times the Isle of Man (happy memories) Lambert and Bangor Bay, Ailsa Craig (Paddy's Milestone) a lone island and bird sanctuary, shaped like a round cake tin, which was passed and repassed. Admiral Lyster came aboard on the 22nd June.

We had been exercising for days when out of the blue came 24 hours leave. It was impossible for me to go home and back in time. I did not fancy staying in Glasgow even if the lads said that Barrowlands Dance Hall was the thing to do in addition to drinking. I decided to get accommodation at a Methodist Holiday Home, Dhalling

Mhor, Kirn. Alan Hislam, Charles Charleston and Stephen Bucknell were interested. I was looking forward to this excursion as I had stayed there in peace time. Leave started in drenching rain and we were soaking. It was worse when we were in the drifter. The usual scramble took place when we drew alongside the Albert Harbour, Greenock, and we tumbled over each other from drifter to drifter in order to reach the jetty. A phone call to Dunoon 234, the spinning of a pitiful yarn of four sailors home from the sea and no home to go to, but with a few hours leave, finally clinched accommodation for us even though they were full of holiday makers.

We took the bus to Gourock. It was still pelting down. A really good dinner at the British Sailors' Society was partaken: new potatoes (yes, new potatoes) roast, peas, followed by prunes and rice and coffee. We had to wait a couple of hours before the *Q.M.* sailed for Dunoon. There was the usual bustle on the quayside: holiday makers standing impatiently, porters pushing trucks laden with luggage, and cars dodging among the milling crowd. There was plenty of shipping near the Tail of the Bank. The *Empress of Scotland* lay at anchor. Light craft, tugs and motor boats scurried around.

We reached Dunoon and walked to Dhalling Mhor in time for tea. We took a stroll along the promenade and returned for supper. At our table sat three undergraduates from Lady Margaret Hall, Oxford. We attended the evening concert with them after which we all went for another stroll along the promenade. Conversation was a sheer delight after our usual moronic topics. And so to bed. What luxury—a feather bed and clean sheets. All too soon came morning. The four of us had breakfasted before the rest of the house was awake. We gave them a rousing Wakey-wakey down each corridor and Charlie-Charlie, and Rise and Shine in our most dulcet tones. No response. Right then: Feet on the Deck: Out of them hammocks: The sun is scorching your eyes out: but we omitted the not so polite ones. Bedroom doors were cautiously opened and

HMS Formidable exercising with destroyers off Gibraltar.
Picture takem from the battleship HMS Rodney. Photo: Imperial War Museum

The finale of a show in the hangar on board HMS Formidable — L. to R: Michael Wilding, Jeanne de Casalis, Beatrice Lillie, John Gielgud, Phyllis Stanley, Edith Evans and Elizabeth Welch — Christmas 1942
Photo: Imperial War Museum

A grand sight for the people of Algiers — HMS Formidable comes right into the harbour and ties up alongside the jetty — 1 June 1943
Photo: Imperial War Museum

Oiling at sea — HMS Formidable & HMS Euryalus.
Photo: Imperial War Museum

Firefighters busy on board HMS Formidable after a Japanese suicide plane had crash-landed on the flight deck — 9 May 1945
Photo: Imperial War Museum

HMS Formidable leading the victorious British Pacific Fleet into
Sydney Harbour — 23 August 1945
Photo: Imperial War Museum

Royal Naval sailors help Australian POWs to board HMS Formidable *which took 1300 repatriates to Sydney from Manila — 5 October 1945*
Photo: Imperial War Museum

Aerial photograph of HMS Formidable returning to Sydney from her special mission of repatriating British and Australians who were imprisoned by the Japanese. — 14 October 1945

Photo: Imperial War Museum.

hurriedly closed on such unmethodical actions.

We caught the 0845 back to Gourock and after a little shopping in Greenock returned to the comforts of *Formidable*. About eighty ratings were adrift.

In the forenoon of the 27th June the lower deck was cleared. The Skipper was to address us. We knew the score. Three ratings under punishment had during the week-end pinched the ship's pinnace, gone ashore and deserted. The pinnace was lost for a few days but found stranded on the Ayrshire coast. The Skipper spoke. He said that there had been no necessity to give us leave but he, and the Commander, had discussed the matter and had decided to take the risk. He had expected some desertions, but not to the extent and numbers who did, over eighty. He said that his shore leave had been spoiled when he returned on Sunday. The Commander, who would take the can, had been ordered to bed for 36 hours. He expressed satisfaction that 95% of the ship's company had returned and then went on to say that the next three weeks would be the hardest we had ever known. However, he had never had an unhappy ship's company, and didn't want one. The Officers and W.O.'s were the best ever, the Commander was the best in the Navy and had gone to great pains to look after our welfare. He knew that stories had been spread and had gone around that the *Formidable* was known as ALTMARK II and men coming on draft had jumped it. He was anxious to know our grievances and was, therefore, going to choose 25 men at random to go to his cabin and express what the dissatisfactions were. No names would be taken and there would be no victimisation. A gangway was cleared for him to pass among the crew and pick 25 men to tell him their grievances and feelings. The following morning Chiefs, and P.O.'s, and Leading Rates were summoned by the Skipper who said that he had listened to the men and that the past would be forgotten and that certain practices such as snooping would cease. During this time I was chatting to an ex-destroyer rating who remarked; "Routine! This bloody ship. Why the one I was on and Divisions had been piped nobody would have known what to do. Colours! Anyone that was passing. Watch ashore! Ratings who had money in their pockets."

On the 30th June Admiral Lyster joined the ship just off Largs. We had been anchoring off Lamlash and the view from the flight deck was superb. Lamlash nestles at the foot of hills, whilst further in the distance, Goatfell and the mountains of Arran could be seen, their jagged edge cutting the sky. The landscape was well wooded although quite good stretches of green rolled down to the Kyles. The coastguard station at Toward Point stood out in its whiteness. Sailing down the Clyde to anchor off Greenock was interesting. The boom was passed at Dunoon and quite good views could be obtained from our port holes of Dunoon, Kirn, Holy Lough, Gourock.

Early one morning I watched the motor cutter being lowered as the ship was coming to anchor off Lamlash. The boat was slung out and skimmed the water which rushed by. The men forward shivered in the biting air. Stokes stood upright by the engine, his oilskins giving him some protection, whilst cox and bowmen waited for the opportune moment for the ropes to be released so the cutter could sheer away. The whole procedure was dangerous and tricky, it demanded perfect timing or the cutter would crash into the ship's side as she took to the water. Looking down through the scuttle I had a view, a picture of swirling white water racing away under the cutter.

On Sunday, 2nd July, we lay off Largs. No wonder it is advertised as Bonny Largs. The resort is backed by low lying Ayrshire hills and is fairly well wooded. It appeared to have no depth, it stretched along the coast with everything being at the front. Two red sandstone churches rise above the shops and houses: one possesses a very graceful spire, but the other is spoiled with a white faced clock. A white-washed shieling stands in loneliness up on the hills.

That afternoon the main attraction of holiday makers was boating. Dozens of row boats nosied around the *Formidable* and the *Indefatigable*. We thumbed lifts from them and offered to sell the carriers. Girls reclining in boats received verbal attention from the crews. During the afternoon a whole battalion of Cadet Corps besieged us.

A draft of thirty odd ratings left at Largs, all were for detention quarters, these being some of the deserters.

We left Largs for Bangor Bay where many American ships were. One which particularly interested us and amused us had a huge painting of a diving bather in swim trunks painted on its bows. From Bangor we sailed to Scapa, but fog considerably delayed us.

There were many near collisions. Engines were put into reverse at times. The mournful sound of the sirens frequently eeried in the whiteness. We arrived at Scapa at 21.00 on the 4th. Shore leave was given on the 5th but I was working. I managed to go ashore on the 7th. Alan, Charlie, Jimmy, Steve, Don and I stepped out on the land of seagulls and islands. We were landed at Gibraltar Pier and strolled through the shanty town and into the open fields. Rows of potatoes were being hoed, cattle grazed in the small spaces their tethers would allow, whilst sheep wandered aimlessly about.

We had tea and cakes at the Church of Scotland Canteen and a game of table tennis. We drifted back to the Fleet Club and had a good meal of bacon and chips. The walls decorated with murals were amusing and interesting: old time sailors dressed in tasselled caps and ringed stockings were playing cards, or saying farewell to buxom wenches or drinking in Spanish cellars, or just drinking, whilst others were chasing each other off the jetty and into the sea. Then we went into the beer hall. Here drinking was for drinking's sake. Matelots, young and old were drinking themselves stupid, maudlin singing, involuntary vomiting. The next place of call was more refreshing, a decent Fleet Club. The one storey building was divided into games, reading, music, quiet games, information rooms. Other rooms included a lounge and a barber's shop. Each room was beautifully decorated and appointed: rugs on the floor, comfortable chairs and settees chintz covered, tasteful prints on the walls which were cream coloured. There was also a library. Good show, Navy.

We made our way back to the pier and gradually the crowds assembled for the waiting drifters. There was the usual tipsy ones who had enjoyed their run ashore but did not know which was their drifter and not caring either. The drifters all left at the same time. They criss-crossed each other as they jockeyed for their course. They always appeared to be on the point of colliding with each other but not doing so. We lurched over the water holding imaginary races with each other across the turbulent waves and tried to shelter from the cross winds.

Back on board and just in time for the end of the ship's concert. McNamara's Band was going full blast with a throaty swing.

S.S.I.—Admiral McGrigor and others came aboard and during the next few weeks we exercised. Exercising still continuing we sailed into the Atlantic where the heavier rollers could be felt. On return to Flotta I had another run ashore. This time I lay down on a grassy bank and in no time I was fast asleep and slept for two solid hours. We put to sea again on the 14th and set course northwards. Buzzes abounded. What fertile imaginations there were. We had to get the Tirpitz which was supposed to be lying in Alten Fjord. The Graf Zeppelin was another contender. Obviously something was afoot. We were off in good company: the carriers *Furious* and *Indefatigable*: battlewagons including the *Duke of York*: cruisers *Jamaica*, *Devonshire* and *Bellona*; and ten destroyers. Others joined us during the night.

The Skipper spoke to us on the 14th July. "The day after tomorrow we shall be attacking enemy units in northern waters. The exercises we will do today and also tomorrow will, therefore, be of the greatest importance. We may be attacked by submarines or dive bombers at any time after tomorrow. You know, as well as I do, that we are not yet fully trained, but if you listen carefully to what I have to say now, you can do quite a lot in the next forty eight hours. Each Officer and man should think carefully and seriously by himself of the exact duties required of him in action and use all his ability to think, reason and find out what exactly is required of him in action. If 1400 men do this conscientiously and thoroughly for 48 hours, the efficiency of the ship would be raised 50%. I wish you good luck."

There was no need to darken ship that night. We had passed into the Arctic Circle. It was as clear as daylight the whole night through. On Sunday, the 16th there was a slight fog and consequently poor visibility. Hammocks of certain ratings were permitted to be slung during the afternoon in order that they may be assured of maximum rest before the action. The Skipper emphasised the need of everyone who could to force themselves to sleep until 16.00, after they had eaten their dinner, especially the air crews and A.H.P. A Service was held in the C Hangar at 18.30. We sang; "Eternal Father, strong to save," and "Praise the Lord ye heavens adore Him." The Skipper read from the Gospel according to St. John. chapter 14, verses 1-7.

At 20.30 we went to Action Stations. Barracudas and Corsairs took off at 22.00 and the first came back at 03.00. During the withdrawal on Monday a lone Barracuda was observed attacking three destroyers. The attack was made below the level of the surrounding hills and in face of much flack. A 1600lb. bomb scored a direct hit in Lang Fjord.

Of course I saw none of the action. I had a few minutes of fresh air on a weather deck at about 02.00. The sea sparkled in the midnight sun and the *Indefatigable* and other ships were as clear and sharp as if it were midday. Two aircraft did not return. I do not know if the operation is successful or not. The *Tirpitz* and other ships had put up a smokescreen and nothing could be seen of them. In fact some aircraft returning had their bombs with them. I believe the f ord had shore batteries every few yards. As a whole we were disappointed with the operation. We anchored at Scapa at 17.30 on the 19th.

Amazing news followed during the next few days. The Japanese Government had resigned and Tojo had been put on the retired list. Better still, an attempt had been made to assassinate Hitler by a group of high ranking officers, even members of his body guard were involved.
On Sunday the C-in-C. Sir—Moore came on board. He told us that we were temporarily attached to the Home Fleet. We embarked aircraft and, in true naval fashion, took them off again immediately. The C-in-C. told us that we were Home Fleet but he was going to London to find out what was going to happen to us. In the meantime we would exercise sharing with the *Indefatigable*'s aircraft, and working up to utmost efficiency.

The 24th brought us a ship's concert. A prize of ten shillings was offered for the best turn. It commenced well and then the usual filthy jokes came to the forefront and equally doubtful singing. The Skipper cleared the lower deck on the 25th and what a hammering he gave the ship's company. His opening words—If anyone thinks that there is going to be any leave he is a fool—were vehemently screamed. He then proceeded to give a long talk upon the necessity for discipline invoking Nelson in so going. The baudiness at the concert had something to do with this dressing down. The ship was demoralised.

At last I had a chance of seeing a film on board, usually I was working when films were shown. In fact I saw two films: The Prisoner of Zenda, and And the Angels Sang. I attended a gramophone recital in the church on Wednesday. The programme was chosen by Jim Slater and was most enjoyable. On Thursday we went to sea and stayed out until Sunday. Fog interfered with the exercises.

I was now detailed to the Bridge Plot. I was instructed by the Schoolmaster in these duties. I thought I would never get the hang of it—so much to do in so short a time. Four hours watch is four hours of intense concentration. I suppose I should be pleased to be chosen for this work, but it is in addition to my other duties. The work is plotting the ship's course on a chart which is placed on a glass topped table. Underneath this is a moving spot of light which is controlled by the ship's gyro and shows the ship's progress. In addition are zig-zags to take into account. These are secret codes which set out alterations to the ship's direction. Instead of moving in a straight line and, therefore, making you an easy target for a submarine to torpedo you, you move in changed directions called legs which are of varying duration and angles. You finish up, however, after some time, say two hours, still on the same mean course. The officer on the bridge will shout down the voice pipe the number of the zig-zag to be followed. You find it in the secret code book and then construct the angles and times of the advances bearing in mind the present line of direction of the ship shown on the gyro before you on the bulkhead. You have to give the officer on the bridge 30 seconds warning of change of direction. He invariably gave you 45 seconds to find the code chosen and construct the zig-zag. Of course they had already done their homework before telling you the change. Was it intended masochism? Working with you in the bridge plot office which is completely blacked out, and at night you work in a red light, is a Radar rating watching his screen for objects at sea which appear as blobs. You report this information to the officer on the bridge and if he so desires these are also plotted on your chart. It is possible to estimate the speed and distance of the object shown on the screen. There is no relaxation. I was now on watch without supervision for the first time. It had been an extremely busy time, more objects than Soft Mick, with instructions from the bridge to record them and give speed and distances. It was a frenetic watch.

Then another voice sounded from a different pipe. It congratulated me and the radar rating on our performance. It was Jimmy the One's voice, the dreaded one. He had a small cabin, not his sleeping cabin, next to the Bridge Plot and while resting on a bunk he had been listening to what was happening on my first sole duty. It is rumoured that he neither slumbered nor slept.

One Sunday afternoon, much later, I had been on the bridge plot and a zig-zag had been in operation for some time. I sang out the next change and watched the gyro turning. It is somewhat strange but when turning to port the ship makes a slight turn to starboard as if to get a leverage to turn to port, and vice versa. On this particular occasion the ship turned the short leverage direction but continued doing so, and instead of steering to port we were moving in a starboard direction. You cannot tell an officer that he is in the wrong, well you can and face the music. I enquired down the voice pipe if we had abandoned the zig-zag. NO. Then shouldn't we be on such and such a course? The ship shuddered and changed direction. On my chart, my guardian angel prompted me, I recorded the conversation with the officer on the bridge. Minutes later the door of the bridge plot room burst open and Jimmy the One swept me to one side so as to examine my chart. His eyes caught the comment I had made on the chart. Without a word he went out on the bridge. I did not see or hear what happened there but learned later that the officer on the bridge had been replaced. Jimmy the One returned. "What would have happened if we had been in convoy, Brown?" "An accident, possibly a ship sunk and lives lost, Sir." "And who would have been to blame?" "The officer on the bridge, Sir." "NO." "Who then, Sir?" "You Brown." "But that isn't fair, Sir. It wasn't my fault." "No Brown, but you were the lowest rating." "But that isn't fair, Sir." "Nothing is fair, Brown." But there was a twinkle in his eye.

Perhaps I had better break off the day to day narrative now that I have mentioned Jimmy the One. He is in command of the lower deck. His name is Lt. Commander J. Byng Frewen, an officer for whom I have the greatest respect. If 100% efficiency is possible then this officer would achieve it. He was strict but fair. He was calm and all seeing. He knew every rating on the lower deck and I

96

would not have been surprised that he knew their numbers as well. He knew what working parties they had been assigned to each morning. Two examples. He might ask a rating if he were in the right working party and he would check up the reply. If it were wrong, then look out. One rating told him he was not in the right party but as he liked painting he had transferred himself to it. He saw that the rating was transferred to that party, then went back and told him that he would check up and see that he was doing a good job, and he did. Another example: we were off the coast of Norway in dense fog. The officer on the bridge came to check my chart plot. He did not agree with my record and gave me a roasting. Things deteriorated. I am sure their record showed us sailing down the Unter den Linden. Jimmy the One was sent for. I believe he was not well at the time and in his cabin. The fog cleared momentarily and without the aid of modern technical help but with a watery sun and a sextant this King's Navigator established the exact position of the ship from the bridge. This is his strength. He came back to the Bridge Plot room and said to me, "Your chart is correct. Carry on." I dare not think what would have happened if I had been wrong.

Regulations appeared on Sunday informing that ratings could apply for transfer to the army. I'm too old. Some of the ship's company are applying. Monday, the 31st. A few incidents lead to the clearing of the lower deck and stokers and leading stokers had another lecture on discipline. They were assembled on the flight deck where a hockey match was in progress. One small stoker was more interested in the match than the lecture, his head was turned away from the Skipper. This was observed and an eye-ball to eye-ball wigging followed. There is an undercurrent feeling boiling. One party has been brought back to the flight deck repeatedly giving them no chance to eat, and when they did the meal was stone cold. They decided that they were not obeying the pipe this time and closed admittance to their mess. The matter was settled by Lt. Commander O'Rorke who left the ship we learned at 01.15. The

97

atmosphere is depressing. I think I'll volunteer for the mines. Cheer up: I had a game of badminton during the dogs and a game of deck hockey.

Sunday morning saw us at Divisions. The D.O. picked me up, I had a spot of cigarette ash on my tie. I wasn't charged. After Divisions the Skipper spoke to us of the new organisation and the necessity of our conforming to it as soon as possible: the irritating conditions under which we'd been working; of lodger squadrons; fog for twenty five days out of thirty four; of our working up for operation; of his request to steam into the Atlantic to exercise and a refusal met with; of our going into the Irish sea in the hope of encountering better weather; of no damage to the *Tirpitz*; but nothing about leave. We anchored in Bangor Bay on Monday at 16.00.

On Tuesday a draft left the ship, these were volunteers for the army. Someone spotted an armed officer today. On Wednesday I got a venomous dressing down from my W.O. I put constructions on his words which were never intended. I listened then asked for a transfer to some other section, Radar, or whatever. He said that I was walking out on a job, had I not any self respect? I stated my case and after a long discussion which commenced like a March wind and ended as a zephyr he said that I could apply to change but that it would not be granted. The Chief said to me afterwards, "You made him crawl."

We put to sea again on Thursday. We cruised round the Irish Sea and about 20.00 steamed northwards on our way to Scapa. There was plenty of shipping about: a fishing fleet, so there was an enormous amount of plotting to do, courses and speeds and more besides were being demanded of us. A shock came down the voice pipe after giving the O.O.W. a particular reading. "A very good plot, Brown." It was Jimmy the One. I think I'll tell my W.O. that.

We closed Action Stations on the 11th and there was no chance of loafing. We had more than that to do. God help us in action. The Minches were passed through during the forenoon and I had a delightful view of the islands and a blue sea dancing in brilliant sunshine. The green hills and brown cliffs made me think of planning a holiday on Skye, and wishing you were climbing the Coolins instead of through hatches and manholes. On Sunday I had a run ashore with Alan. The afternoon was delightfully fresh and we strolled round Flotta. It is not very interesting but the pastel shades of the scenery were most pleasant. A fair amount of shipping was off Lyness, they looked like toy ships in a sea of blue plastic. We went to a concert in the evening: Len Goosens, oboe: Eric Greene, tenor: Mary Lind, soprano: and Ivor Newton at the piano. They played classical items in a popular manner. I enjoyed the Elizabethan madrigals sung by Eric Greene and Mary Lind and Ivor Newton's playing of Bach's Jesu Joy of Man's Desiring.

The Russian Fleet had invited the British ships' companies, or was it the other way round, to a social evening and volunteers were invited from each ship. Alan and I volunteered. The Social was held in the Ratings' Bar, not too good a place, but nevertheless suitable. Refreshments were provided: Sandwiches, sausage rolls. teddy 'oggins, jam tarts, cakes and beer. We were soon spread out among our allies. Most of the Russians spoke a few words of English and so, although there was conversation, it was difficult. The evening opened with The King and the Russian Anthem, not the Internationale. Most of our new friends came from Leningrad but were not in the siege. They were delightfully jolly and charming. If Vanya and I were not able to understand each other we dragged in Feodor seated across the table. And so it went on: very little understood of what had been spoken but a lot understood that we were friends and allies and proud to be so. Our first three toasts were to Joe Stalin. We exchanged souvenirs and I got a cap badge with the hammer and sickle superimposed. Unfortunately we had to leave early but I'll always remember these polite Russian sailors, especially those from the *Archangel*, known to us as the Rusty Rouble.

The next few days we exercised. The Allies launched an invasion of Southern France on the 15th.

Towards 2130 on the 17th the *Archangel*, previously the *Royal Sovereign* left anchorage and as she passed us we heard resounding cheers. We cleared lower decks except for those already turned in, and as the *Archangel* passed us we responded with cheers which echoed across the Flow. My singing of the Internationale was a solo lost in the wind.

The Skipper spoke to us that we were to proceed to sea the following morning the 19th. We were to make another attack on the *Tirpitz* and anything else that might be there. There were to be several attacks and we might be away for a fortnight. Five aircraft carriers were to take part in the several operations planned. We might go away for a few days to re-fuel destroyers and return to make other attacks. Submarines were in the vicinity during the night. It became colder. Heavier seas and rain storms were encountered. We still steered northwards and during the middle watch on the 20th we passed into the Arctic Circle. On Sunday and Monday we trailed our coats along the Norwegian coast from north of Hammerfest to south of Trondheim. Submarine scares occurred and depth charges reverberated. The attack was to have taken place on Monday forenoon but at 23.00 on Sunday it was postponed for a day. It is now 21.00 on Monday. I haven't long since come off watch. Depth charging continues. The Fleet is moving quickly. Bows are snow white manes. The sky is like gun metal and the sea an irridescent shade. We were at Action Stations on Tuesday; long wearisome hours from 06.00 to 00.20 the next morning.

We got our aircraft off much quicker than the *Indefatigable*, but our pilots did not find the target and dropped the bombs into the sea. The Flying Dutchmen off the *Indefatigable* scored a hit on the *Tirpitz* and later on shot down eleven enemy planes. Radar stations were also hit. Jerry hit the Escort Carrier, *Nabob*. She got under her own steam much later. A frigate was sunk. We sailed westwards splitting into two forces and at a comfortable distance destroyers were oiled.

I came up on the weather deck for a breath of fresh air. We were about thirty miles from the Lofoten Isles which loomed black against a pale sky. The caps of the hills were snow covered and there was an impression of glaciers sweeping down to the sea. Accurate results were not observed by *Formidable* due to smoke but two doubtful hits were estimated by Barracudas. As regards the Corsairs there was definitely a near miss and one possible hit on the *Tirpitz*. A seaplane base was attacked and two seaplanes and huts were destroyed. The *Norge* was hit and an ammunition ship was blown up. At Bukta the hangar runway and control tower were hit. A flack ship, a large merchantman and a destroyer were left burning in Lang Fjord. Another flack ship was left burning and another at the entrance of Oho blew up. A flack ship east of Silden was sinking. Four corsairs from the *Formidable* failed to return. One was forced down into the sea astern of the ship and the pilot was picked up. The *Furious* reported that the target was completely obscured by a smoke screen but was located by gun flashes and cordite smoke. No hits were seen. *Indefatigable* reported one hit with a 500 lb. bomb from a Hellcat on the port side of the bridge, and another possible hit.

The general report of the C-in-C. was that considerable damage had been done: airfields, radar stations, destroyers, flack ships, one merchant ship and at least ten enemy aircraft. Owing to the clouds in the first attack it had not been possible to inflict major damage to the *Tirpitz* but it was possible that she had received at least three hits from the low flying aircraft, but these would not have put her out of action. It would, therefore, be necessary to provide cover for the returning Russian convoy.

We proceeded westwards to oil destroyers in readiness for an attack upon the *Tirpitz*. Tuesday, the 29th was the day of the next attack. All I can report is long wearying hours at Action Stations, excessive weariness, and a thick headache. Conditions on board are far superior to those on destroyers. I would be a wreck if I were serving on them. A preliminary report of the attack was made on Wednesday: nothing definite, possible hits and near misses. Consequently we had to provide cover for the convoy which I learned was 150 miles east of Bear Island and was crashing through wild waters at eight knots.

We made Scapa on Saturday and left for Rosyth later in the day passing under the Firth of Forth Bridge about 16.00. This day was the fifth anniversary of the outbreak of war and a Service was held in the hangar in the forenoon.

The first leave party left today on a six days leave. The Skipper informed us during the forenoon that our stay at Rosyth was limited. We were due to leave on 15th September which was the day the second leave party returned. We were bound for the Far East.

I went on leave on the 9th again for home comforts, at 14.30. We changed at Waverley Station, Edinburgh, took the connection to Princess Street, changed at Carlisle and Preston, arrived at Exchange, Manchester at 00.30, managed to get a naval bus going to Oldham, and opened our front door at 01.30. I should have mentioned the solitary girl in our compartment who handed round her bottle of whisky which we duly consumed.

I won't talk about the next six days of freedom spent at home. I left at 12.30 on Thursday, the 14th, caught the 14.00 from Exchange, changed at Wigan, entrained for Carlisle, waited there for a connection which did not arrive, so moved on to Carstairs for the connection to Edinburgh. Railway travel!!! Oh, well there's a war on. I arrived on board at 12.00 on Friday, the 15th. We left Rosyth during the night and stayed a few hours at Scapa that night. The Skipper spoke to us on the 16th and told us we were on our way out East, and our first stop would be Gibraltar.

On Sunday we sailed through the Hebrides, North Channel, and Irish Sea. This was a new route and showed us the value of the army's progress in France. On passing the Isle of Man during the middle watch, the light of the Wireless Station was blazing away. We sailed westwards south of Cork then altered course and proceeded through the Bay of Biscay.

At dinner time on Wednesday a Corsair crashed, tearing away the aerials and passing our mess scuttles. I saw the pilot dive through the fuselage just before the wreckage submerged. He was picked up by a destroyer. We arrived at Gibraltar on Thursday, the 21st at 17.00. It's getting warm.

Friday and shore leave. A few of us went to Catalan Bay to swim. Here the Portuguese fishermen cottages lie away from a delightful beach. We had a meal and then went to the Royal where "French for Love" was being played.

We went ashore the following evening and swam at Eastern Beach which we thought not as pleasant as Catalan Bay. It was spoiled by seaweed. A splendid meal at the Winter Gardens followed by broaching a bottle of wine. As the theatres were full we did a sedate pub crawl. From the open bars we watched the constantly moving throng on Main Street and the senoritas leaning from the balconies. Of course Jack had filled the bars with song, step dancing on tables and platform, and nautch girl miming.

I had a full day's duty on Sunday the 24th so was excused Divisions which Admiral Burroughs attended. Speeches were made on the reallocation of man power, demobilisation and pay to the Forces in the Far East. I had an operation on the 24th for haemorrhoids. Very disgusting and painful. I will not recount the conversation of the Canadian Lieutenant Doctor and the Sickbay Orderly who did the operation, which was done on board. Certainly funny, but far from polite dinner conversation. My W.O. had a similar operation but his was done in hospital. I was padded up with cotton wool, slept on the iron deck as it was

103

too painful to sleep in my hammock, and continued working.

Most runs ashore at Gibraltar are similar but a great improvement had been effected since we were last here. The Y.M.C.A. had opened an excellent canteen and lounge: reading, writing and games rooms: restaurant: balconies; and flat roof where you could sunbathe. Here you could buy excellent meals and snacks. We invariably finished our meals with bananas and grapes when we dined here. The lounge was large and had a high domed roof painted as an open sky and showing a balustrade on which plants climbed and cherubs floated in mid air. We saw many good shows in the lounge. The first one was somewhat intellectual called "Voices on the Rock" an evening of poems and music written and composed by ratings serving on the Rock. There was a Free and Easy Night with items by Servicemen. One I saw was as good a show I have ever seen and was not rehearsed. The two piano accompanists Jimmy Cross a Flying Officer, and a civilian, were brilliant. During this time I saw the Tower Players give "Wind and the Rain" at the Engineers Hall. The play takes place in the digs of medical students in Edinburgh.

On Saturday the South African Ensa Show, "Sundowners" entertained us aboard. They were the best show I have seen. The African songs they sang were tuneful.

The following day there was a church parade to the Methodist Church. I had shore leave in the afternoon and went to the Y.M.C.A. and slept. Afterwards from the roof I watched a cricket match taking place on the barrack square in Alameda Gardens. After a good meal I attended a gramophone recital with works by Tchaikovsky, Rossini, Gounod, Weber, Mozart and Bach: Invitations to the Waltz, Ballet Music from Copellia, Valtz from Sleeping Beauty, Overture to Algiers, Eine Kleine Nachtmusic, Ave Maria sung by Gigli, Gounod's setting with a background of a theme by Bach, Swan Lake music, and Faust Ballet.

On the 10th we moved to the detached mole. This meant our being able to use the heads on board instead of the foul smelling pre-privy efforts on the dock side. After 200 years on the Rock why has British Administration still such atrocities as these primitive toilets similar to the Casbah? But then the toilets at Rosyth and Belfast are equally bad.

Tuesday, 11 October. We sailed with H.E. the Governor, Sir Eastwood and his Lady, and Admiral Burroughs but had to return in the early afternoon owing to engine trouble. The following day the Skipper confirmed that the central engine was beyond repair and remedy could not be effected under three and a half months. We could, however, proceed with two engines and obtain 36 knots which would be sufficient for 90% of the flying demands. Three avenues were then open to us: go home and have a refit: go on with the two engines working; or return home and become part of the Home Fleet so as to release another carrier to take our place. He had no idea which course would be taken, or some other course, as the matter was being considered by the Admiralty. In the meantime no one should jump to the conclusion that we were going home as we might be disappointed. The Captain stated that he would keep us informed of all developments and that no mention must be made of the breakdown in our letters home. On the 14th we were told that the Admiralty had decided that the repairs would be done at Gibraltar. Consequently many of the ship's hands who had engineering experience were roped in to do the work. This went apace: drilling, drawing, stripping, tallying, piling, and all the multifarious activities connected with the removal of the central engine. Arc lights dazzled the flight deck and ratings sweated to remove the offending engine. All this had repercussions throughout the ship. We went on 24 hour watchkeeping and leave was drastically cut.

On the 17th work slowed down as the essential machinery would not arrive before the 1st November, and we would not proceed on our way before December.

As a consequence of cessation of work on the engines the powers that be strained every nerve to find activities for the lower deck. Training classes started with a vengeance, route marches followed, sport blossomed, except for our branch which now attempted to reduce arrears of work. In the meantime we went back to the dry dock which meant that once more we became votaries at the shrine of Hygeia.

News came through on the 29th October of the American Navy's terrific victory over the Japanese Fleet in the Pacific; of 60 ships the Japs now had only two which remained unscathed or not sunk. The RAF too had a good time scoring a direct hit on the elusive foe the *Tirpitz*.

The machinery with certain exceptions arrived on the 1st November. The latest buzz is that we will not be ready before the New Year. On a fleeting shore leave I saw an exceptionally good play "Winterset" by Maxwell Anderson.

For November use the word Entertainment. There was a curious reaction to this. Admittedly everything was being done to entertain us but somehow we felt we were wasting time. We couldn't proceed to sea and the seamen had not enough work to fill the day, hence, something had to be done. Idle hands, etc. I think entertainment interfered with the work of our department but we had to attend instructional films, runs up the Rock (yes run, with officers posted at strategic points to observe) swimming, etc. Out of hours were badminton, soccer, tennis, tug of war, shows in the hangar, uckers, table tennis, hare and hounds, deck hockey, deck tennis, quizzes, and nearly a dance. The dance was arranged for November 25th but it was rumoured that bogus tickets were being sold in Spain, so the dance was cancelled for security reasons. A dance was eventually arranged and took place on the 2nd December. The ship was transformed. The hangar deck was scrubbed with wire brushes until it shone. Ensigns and bunting were draped on the bulkheads, shrubs and ferns gave a palm court effect. A diver's suit stood stiffly to attention and reminded you of a suit of armour. A huge crown had been constructed of wood and studded with coloured lights. In the forward lift well was a small rockery out of which plashed coolly a fountain. The water gurgled its way through the ferns to the scuppers. An outspread parachute of yellow silk took the form of an electric light standard. In the after lift well you could try your rifle skill at shooting at clay pipes, or putt a golf ball into a bath—some outrageous putts were displayed unworthy of St. Andrews, especially by those who had been ashore and had returned not exactly in a sober condition. The effect of your voice on a beam of light could be seen and workings of an aircraft inspected. The tent of a landing wireless set became a fortune teller's tent. Commander Douglas, of oriental appearance, yellow skin and small of stature, was attired in a turban and a flowing robe. He read palms and his imagination knew no bounds. I was told that I had heart trouble and would come to a terrible death, and have one child. Whether I died under the terrible circumstances of acquiring a child was not certain. Dart stalls did a roaring trade while the P.M.O. on the hoop-la stall always had a crowd around him. There was, of course, dancing. Unfortunately, although the Wrens turned up in good numbers considering their strength on the Rock, there were far too few of them and, consequently, every dance had to be an excuse-me. If you managed to dance half a dozen steps before relinquishing your partner you were indeed fortunate. Of course, there were a few matelot couples exhibiting the most novel steps. The Wrens put on a floor show—a syncopated horn-pipe and a Hawaiian tableau. Tables were loaded with sandwiches, cakes, minerals and tea. It was a magnificent evening and all too soon it ended. A ship's dance in peace time must be a wonderful affair.

On Sunday I attended Providence Chapel and the communion service following.

During our enforced active inactivity a few debates had been arranged. One debate was "War degrades humanity."

It was opposed by one of the officers. I spoke for it and perhaps cheated in that I used someone, I forget who it was, who stated that the first casualty in war is truth. I enlarged on this theme, and was well received, and it was picked up time and again by speakers on the platform to which I was invited by Jimmy the One, the chairman for the debate. I declined. I think I had said enough. The motion was passed overwhelmingly.

The dockyard police gave us a preview of their forthcoming concert. It was an excellent evening's entertainment, good music, orchestral and vocal. The Miserere from Il Travatore was marvellously sung and also a scene from the Spanish Opera, Marina, was exceptionally good.

I attended a novices boxing tournament at the RAF New Camp and enjoyed the bouts immensely. Yes there was plenty of amusement, and I lay stress on it, because you cannot make work interesting, and there was plenty of that.

I went to the Sick-bay on the 4th and was put on light duties. I had pains in the chest and although the X-ray treatment was considered they tried clinical treatment with radiant heat.

News from Greece and Italy was very disturbing. In Athens the left-wing groups, who had risked their lives during the German occupation, were refused permission to march through the streets of Athens. They did march and were fired on. Fourteen were killed and over a hundred wounded. Fighting flared up the following day between the rival factions and British troops were used to fight the partisan left wingers. Admittedly, we do not know the whole truth but it beggars belief that the people who fought the hardest for the liberation of their country are getting a raw deal now that their land is liberated from German oppression. In Italy the British Government refuse to recognise the liberal Count as Foreign Secretary despite the fact that for years he resisted Mussolini and Fascism and went into exile. But we recognise Bonomi's Government, also Bodolio, Crown Prince Umbert, and other leaders of Fascism who resisted us until they were defeated, and would have had no mercy if they had won. Had they not boasted that they had taken part of the bombing of London? For what are we fighting?

The week 8th to 15th December, 1944. YMCA Drama Festival. I saw Shaw's "St. Joan": X=O by John Drinkwater: A.P.Herbert's "Two Gentlemen of Soho": and J.J.Bell's "Thread of Scarlet". On Friday I joined the Toc H Outing. This was a visit to the tunnels in the Rock and was lead by Major Williams, the engineer in charge. We saw tunnels being excavated, drilling for the gelignite holes, blasting, etc. Most regiments had personnel working in the Rock and there was a number of Italian Pioneers. There is no silica in the Rock and hence no silicosis. Major Williams informed that the men were extremely healthy because of the calcium. The men were white with the powder, their faces looked clownish in the electric light. The noise of the drills, the rumble of the trucks as they jumped along the lines, and the clatter of the automatic shovels as they threw the broken rock into the trucks, were deafening. Provision had been made for workshops, food dumps, dormitories, ammunition spaces and for every eventuality in the case of the Rock's being bombarded. A most interesting evening although I was disappointed that we did not see St. Michael's caves and lakes.

On Monday the Supply and Secretarial Branch held a dance at 51, Line Wall Road. The Assembly Rooms were not large. They had been decorated with bunting and the verandah had been pressed into service as the bar. As usual there were a few under the weather as time rolled by, which led to very few of them having their own caps in which to return to the ship. The earlier ones to leave must have slammed on the first headgear they came to and staggered into the street. Shipwards bound we picked up one of our mess wearing in sedate majesty a P.O.'s cap which, not only covered his head, but covered half his face. Having got him in tow we stumbled into another on hands and knees searching dazedly for his false teeth. By his side was another inebriated one fast asleep on the pavement. We did our best to awaken him but only succeeded in getting him to vomit over himself. With the aid of M.P.'s we managed to carry him to the Picket House where we had to leave him as we would have been adrift. Coming on board we found two in their hammocks absolutely out to the wide and fully dressed including shoes. We removed their footwear. Two more were prostrate on the deck. We undressed them and put them in their hammock. During the night one of the drunks fell out of his hammock and broke a collar bone. What a wind up!

Back to the dance and what happened there. There were some of our officers and Jimmy the One, and a few Wrens. Jock McCall, always irrepressible, and seeking ways of our getting more of a share of dance partners, we not being officers, told one of the Wren Officers that we had one of the baronetcy in our mess. He proceeded to introduce Duggie, as Sir James Duggie, K.C.B. of Huntley Hall, Nairn. The Wrens who up till then had hardly noticed us, fell for it and gushed around. As we now danced with them they thought how wonderful democracy was. McCall had told the story that Duggie was a banker, actually he was a bank clerk, and he had cleared up quite a lot of money on the Stock Exchange. Duggie was popular in excelsis.

One high note of the dance was that Jimmy the One would give us a demonstration of the Boston Two Step much to his surprise. He was sporting enough to oblige. He flew round the floor as light of foot as anyone could be. The applause was so great he had to give an encore. How many more talents has this man?

The next important item was the Children's Party held on board on the 23rd December. About 300 children were invited from Line Wall Road School; they were accompanied by their teachers. In the hangar swings had been rigged and see saws. Walt Disney cartoons were shown continuously. Flying suits turned inside out were ideal for dressing seamen as bears who gave rides on their backs. The bears were very popular and at times were crushed down under the weight of a dozen children, scrambling on their backs. Side shows were kept busy and musical chairs were never ending. The jeeps never lacked for customers, the children commandeered them and the trailers. The lift well was besieged for rides to the flight deck were in constant demand. Children raced all over the hangar and took complete charge of the sailors and lead them sedately to all places of interest. Never were great hulking men so much under the control of youngsters. Father Christmas rounded off the party by stepping out of a Corsair as it was brought down from the flight deck; I think the crew got the greatest pleasure, but it might have been a draw.

Christmas Day, 1945 Rain. Pipe down at 09.00.

The messes were decorated and ours was festooned with streamers and greenery. A cardboard pub, the Admiral Benbow, Proprietor, Jack Dusty was built in the hammock netting. A mural of the Rock with a galleon scudding by hung on the bulkhead. Coloured lights gave a joyous radiance. The menu for the day was:-

---

BREAKFAST
Corn Flakes.   Mixed Grill.
Rolls   Marmalade.

DINNER
Tomato Cream Soup
Roast Turkey & Stuffing.   Boiled Ham.
Potatoes   Cauliflower   Peas
Christmas Pudding and White Sauce
Apples   Oranges and Mixed Nuts

TEA
Christmas Cake   Mince Pies

SUPPER
Cold Roast Legs of Pork   Pickles

Cheese   Biscuits
AND A BOTTLE OF BEER EACH

Everything was superbly cooked and was delicious. We had ourselves bought apples, oranges, sultanas, almonds, bananas, grape fruit.

I went to Providence Chapel in the morning with Jack Larkin of Radar and had communion. In the afternoon I went ashore to the YMCA. Everything was on the house. I had an excellent turkey tea and I enjoyed the concert at night.

The ship's masthead was decorated, and also the aerials and the gangway. After 09.30 dress was your own affair. Consequently it was not surprising to see stokers dressed as Engineer Officers and even the Jaunty, sideboys as chefs, and as many fancy dresses as you can imagine.

A Rounds Party toured the ship very unsteadily, complete with pseudo Officer of the Day and R.P.O. Officers were dragged from the Ante Room and their cabins. Caps disappeared from the Ward Room and many a lower rating had well braided headgear.

I saw two good films: "Song to Remember": the life story of Chopin. I must try and read something by George Sandes, and I also saw "The Adventures of Mark Twain."

On New Years Eve I got extended shore leave to attend the Watch Night Service at Providence Chapel. There was an exceptionally good number of service personnel in the congregation. It was good to sing "Come let us anew" to the old tune. As we came out of chapel the minister greeted each one of us with a Happy New Year. The first one to do this after the minister was a soldier from my district Newton Heath. Ships in the basin were blowing sirens and whistles. Coloured lights were rocketing over the harbour, a brilliant fireworks display. Apparently one of the customs at Gibraltar at the start of the New Year is to break glass. Bottles came flying from windows and spangled the pavements. It was dangerous walking back to the ship.

I had the opportunity of looking over a submarine, the *Vampire*. Quarters were very confined: one stride took you down from the Ward Room right into the galley. Certainly close quarters. I did not envy them. A torpedo man from Edinburgh showed us over the submarine. He was full of praise for it, caressed the torpedoes, spoke lovingly of the periscope, explained why the *Thetis* was sunk and showed us the Davis apparatus and escape chamber.

1945

We sailed on New Years Day, 1945. Once more we were experiencing a working programme. We fell in for leaving harbour, coming to attention and standing at ease for over an hour, whilst the tugs coaxed us away from the jetty. We exercised in the Mediterranean where even yet submarines were still lurking. In fact a merchant ship received a packet just outside the Straits but managed to get back into harbour.

On Friday, the *Wolverine* was drawing away from us, and we could see two young porpoises keeping just ahead of her bows, frequently jumping out of the sea.

I should have had the morning watch on Saturday but I was not shaken and when Wakey-wakey sounded I froze. I couldn't believe it but, as the bugle persisted, my lashing went round my hammock for the seventh time before my feet touched the deck. I hurried to the bridge and luckily nothing had happened; we were during a transition period and at that time were one over complement for the watch, and I had not been missed. There were more panics to follow during the remainder of the watch but these will be forgotten.

We returned for a brief spell at Gibraltar during which I saw a Forces Pantomine at the Theatre Royal, and a South African Concert Party at the Garrison. On Friday Jim Barnes of Oswaldtwistle came aboard and invited us over his ship, the *Stalker*, for the evening. We stayed until 22.30. Saturday, the 13th was fixed for the H.P. Trials. Everything was ready and we did not stir from the mole. We sailed on Sunday the 14th, and the engines appeared to stand up to the test. Night manoeuvres were held. There were U-boat activities and one ship was sunk and another attacked. Our escort destroyers were *Vigilant* and *Saumarez*.

114

Warsaw fell on the 17th. This time it was to the U.S.S.R.

The sea was too rough to enter Alexandria harbour on the 19th so we cruised around and had extra flying operations. Similarly on the 20th and 21st. This Sunday proved disastrous. Three kites were lost and what was worse the pilots did not escape. We then entered Alexandria at 16.00. There had been no calming of the sea when we entered, no difference than when we were told that it was not possible to enter.

I got my first shore run on Tuesday the 23rd. A.T.L.C. was used as the liberty boat. We saw the usual sights in the dockyard, natives whose dress is indescribable and filthy. Many appeared to be covered in rags sewn together. One native was manacled to a policeman and seemed to be enjoying the procedure. Outside the dockyard similar bundles of animated rags assailed you with offers to shine your shoes, tell your fortunes, sell you at fantastic prices cheap jewellery, cut your hair, cut and sew you a suit, invite you to taste the beer, have your photograph taken, and of course, sell you dirty postcards and books.

We booked bed and breakfast at the United Services Club, we couldn't find the St. Andrew's Hostel. Then we shopped and found that the prices were exorbitant. I wanted to buy some silk dress lengths but they were asking £4.10.0d for 3½ metres. I bought three pairs of silk stockings instead. We had coffee and cakes, and ice cream and fruit at the Club, and returned much later for a meal followed with ice cream and fruit. An Ensa Show followed and was quite good. Before returning to the Club we had a few John Collinses, Gin Slings, and de Kuypers Curacao. Delicious. Someone was sick during the night but fortunately there was a mosaic floor. A shuffling bemuffled figure awoke us at 06.00. We could not face breakfast. The streets were quite lively at that hour. Bundles of rags were purchasing their breakfasts at numerous dirty bakeries. Breakfast seemed to consist of large thin cakes or rolls. Squalor was everywhere. It was cold and wet waiting at the jetty where there were ubiquitous vendors of cold lemonade and fruit. One pathetic youngster of about six years of age was trying to sell eggs.

Once again there is flooding outside my store, oil this time. It had oozed its way in and soaked everything to a depth of 6″. It was indescribable and I had the unenviable task of trying to get everything back into reasonable condition. There was the task of removing the oil and logging stores which had been ruined: valves, motors, etc. When I had finished that I had the seemingly endless job of ridding myself of the sticky substance. The pipes did not reach down here and consequently I did not hear the rum call. It was my turn to draw the rum for the mess. I was five minutes late. What a terrific bottling I received from Mr. Branch. And to make matters worse I did not say Sir. By such words are wars won. I went ashore to draw stores from 45 shed. I was on my own checking as fast as I could and attempting at the same time to see that Arabs did not pinch anything. It did not amuse me to see from another ship a party come to draw stores: it consisted of one Commander (S), two chiefs, P.O.'s. three leading rates and two assistants, besides a working party. I had a bigger load than they had.

I went ashore in the afternoon with Alf, Johnny and Edgar. We booked beds at the United Services Club then fixed up with, would you believe it, a Dragoman (no.12) with the name of SPUD MURPHY to drive us round Alexandria in his taxi. I had done the run before: Pompey's Palace, Karmous, King Farouk's Palace, the Nile, Native Quarters, and the Cornische. We tried to enter the Abbas Mosque but as it was Friday this was not possible. It is a comparatively new mosque and had been built by the previous King, Fuah. It is really beautiful and possesses delicate tracery and elaborate domes. A huge door is inlaid with copper, but all round was squalor. We returned to the Fleet Club for a meal and afterwards went shopping. More de Kuypers Curacao and finished up at the Rialto to see "Standing Room Only". The show commenced at 21.39 and finished at 23.45. We made our way back to Mohamet Ali Square, and so to bed. What might have been an ugly scene was averted. A lone matelot was surrounded by shouting natives in a side street. What had happened, I don't know, possibly his fault, so we escorted him back to the main street, where he left us.

At 06.00 the following morning we made our way back to the docks. The streets were alive with the chattering street cars. Bakeries were emitting their peculiar odours. Strange foods were being cooked on the pavements. Humanity and cats took an even chance at the garbage heaps. *Formidable* was flashing up when we saw her. We sailed at 09.15 and were off Port Said during the dogs.

On Sunday the 28th we sailed through the Suez Canal. I did not see the statue of de Lessops at the entrance but had a good view of the water front of Port Said as we were only a few yards away from it. Here were the commercial houses. An electric sign indicated the theatre and dance hall, whilst an advertisement invited you to spend your holidays in the Swiss Alps.

I thought that the canal would have been wider. There were straight stretches between white sand dunes. Camels and dromedaries mixed with the lorries on the adjacent roadway. Stations, camps, including some for prisoners of war, were dotted along the road. Ismailia, on Lake Timsah, was fresh and cool. Besides modern bulidings it possesses an excellent plage. Of course there were many passes from the crowded flight deck to the lonely sentries along the route. Perhaps the best one was to a lonely soldier, on sentry with nothing but sand dunes stretching to the horizon. "Have you heard the news? Queen Victoria's dead?." We anchored in the Bitter Lakes for the night. This is necessary as there is only room for one way traffic and, therefore, the traffic has to be controlled.

We entered the Gulf of Suez at about 09.00 on the 29th January and late in the day I had a good view of Mount Sinai. There is a similarity along the Red Sea of rock

117

formations approaching a symmetry of design. The sun sank rapidly colouring the sky with pastel shades of green, blue, yellow, pink, and transforming the clouds of white into delicate hues. During the middle watch on Wednesday I prostrated myself, we were passing Mecca. Aden loomed into view on Thursday, 1st February, and we anchored about 17.00. This barren rock, a volcanic rock, was dappled sepia. I spotted a small mosque among the jumbled buildings. A few native craft nosied around manned by spindle legged natives. Many of them salaamed seemingly to the *Formidable*.

The voyage across the Arabian and Indian Oceans was uneventful. Twilight was short, and the sunsets were magnificent. It is impossible to describe the riot of colours which invades the sky as the sun sinks rapidly. Molten gold runs beserk among greens, blues, reds, yellows, and many other colours. We had an alarm, however, "Man overboard" one night. Pipes screamed, "Sentry throw lifebuoy with colour flares aft." "Sentry replace new lifebuoy." "Commander report to the bridge when this is done." Meanwhile the destroyers searched the water with lights. There was a check the following morning but nobody was missing. Possibility, someone sleeping on the cable deck had had a nightmare.

At sea our mess had the use of the starboard after pocket for slinging billet. It was refreshing to emerge from the sweltering heat between decks and strip off in the dark of the weather deck and climb into your hammock. The breeze gently rustled your blanket and the hammock swayed soothingly. It was the utmost pleasure to doze off with the stars blinking down on you and sea loping past.

There was ceremonial entry into Colombo, Ceylon. The low coast line stretched as far as the eye could see. Palm trees grew in profusion. As we sailed into the harbour native craft eddied around filled with a dusky crew. Some of the boats resembled a log of wood, some were outriggers. I managed shore on the third day. Saturday, the 10th. There are

118

many good commercial buildings; the Times of Ceylon had a really handsome edifice. We were assailed by rickshaw drivers but we preferred to walk. Hitch hiking was favoured and we got a lift to the Fleet Club. This was a one-storey building in colonial style. In front of it were lawns and flower gardens with gladioli of vivid colours and standing four feet high. At the back were parched lawns and a banyan tree. I bought a pair of book ends at the Club which were made of king ebony and were shaped as elephants. A further lift took us to Mount Lavinia which is a lovely bathing beach, a white crescent of sand fringed by palm trees, many of which grew obliquely possibly the action of the monsoon during their growth. Bathing and surf riding were in full swing. A couple of beach combers tagged onto us and persuaded us to visit the nearby village where girls were making lace. The machines were primitive with cardboard drums with needles projecting. The lace was neatly made although coarse. An electric railway ran along the coast with modern stream lined coaches. The natives here are far cleaner than those in Egypt and furthermore were not for everlastingly pestering you. We got a lift back to town from Mount Lavinia, which is seven miles out, from a Dutch sailor in a taxi who would not accept anything from us in payment for the ride. He had been out east for eight years. His time had elapsed when war broke out and he had been transferred to the Dutch Navy. His home was in Rotterdam and his family were in German hands. In Mount Lavinia is a Methodist Church with services in English at 06.30 and in Singhalese at 17.30. At Colpetty I saw another Methodist Church, two Dutch Reformed Churches and, of course, St. Andrew's Church of Scotland. The bungalow of the Bishop of Colombo was superb.

Monday the 11th February we left Colombo and sailed for Trincomalee. The harbour here is formed of well wooded coves. There are palm trees and what was delightful were the pink, yellow and red flowers of the tulip tree. The place is small and poor. The shops are mostly made of plaited palm leaves while the goods are cheap and of inferior quality. There is an open drainage system which gives off a far from pleasant odour. The Law Courts were a bungaloid growth. A few shops were closed for the Chinese New Year, February 15-17. I liked one shop's sign "McIsmail" whilst another notice I found interesting was "Village Headman". I saw a few ravens, their blue-black feathers and long beaks were fascinating. A Methodist Canteen with open verandah invited us. I looked twice at the notice board—Service in English 09.30. Service in Tamil 17.30. There is a good bathing beach with a sandy shore at Trincomalee. After a good look round the village we went to the Fleet Club and enjoyed our allowance of one bottle of Australian lager. Frances Day was at the Club and we saw part of the show before queuing up in the pens to return back on board.

In all the clubs and cafes in Colombo and Trincomalee were electric fans shaped like a propeller of an aeroplane suspended from the ceiling, just like you see in the films depicting Indian Club life. We returned to Colombo arriving on the 20th. Here was the usual panic of storing ship and again leave to our watch seems to suffer every time. It all depends on when you reach harbour. I was now relieved of my watchkeeping duties on the Bridge Plot except for Action Stations. It was pleasing to know that Jimmy the One was reluctant to agree to this change, and more so to be stopped by him and thanked personally for my duties there. I was immediately put on cypher duties, something more to learn.

We left Colombo on the 22nd and our next destination was Fremantle. Action Stations on the 23rd. Friday from 07.40 until 15.15. I was now in the Lower Steering position. Here is a duplicate of the bridge plot, in case that is put out of action. This is deep down in the ship and somewhat suffocating. You enter through a hatch which is secured from the outside on the deck above. You descend ladders to enter. There is a continual clanging of bells as the

Quartermaster obeys instructions from the bridge through a voice pipe for the helm wheel to be revolved so that the ship can alter course.

That evening the Ambassador accompanied by underwater police from the Court of King Neptune arrived on board. They climbed over the brow, a fanfare of trumpets sounded. The Undersea Police cleared a passageway with their truncheons. The Ambassador then read the address of the intended visit by King Neptune on the following day when we would be crossing the equator.

On Saturday, the 27th, two huge canvas baths were erected on either side of a platform rigged on the flight deck. King Neptune and Queen Aphrotite (not Aphrodite) with Police, Barbers and Court Officials arrived on board at 13.00 and set up their court on the platform. They summoned the Skipper to appear before them, also the Commander and many Officers, whose crimes were read out and honours bestowed on them. Then the barbers got to work with flour, paste ánd huge wooden razors on their victims. They seated the victims on ducking stools, poured paste over them and released a catch on the back of the chair. The chair swung backwards and the victims were hurled into a bath of water where bears waited to duck them.

Some received a severe ducking and were sentenced to be thrown into the Port and Starboard baths. After a while others joined in and it became a free for all. Everyone was clambering on the platform, the whole of the Court and Police were flung into the baths, whilst those on the flight deck were acting similarly. Hose pipes were turned on the bridge which was stormed. Sleepers were dragged from their messes and flung in, a particularly good prey was anyone fully dressed and dry. I had taken the precautions and was wearing only bathing trunks. This, by the way, was The Ceremony of the Crossing of the Line.

Monday, the 26th and Action Stations. Three aircraft were hopping in and out of the clouds. As we were within 500

121

miles of Japanese bases precautions were necessary. The 4.5's opened fire, but soon we secured. Apparently it was not aircraft and so a wit pinned these lines on the notice board the following day:

TWINKLE, TWINKLE LITTLE STAR, OUR 4.5s WON'T REACH THAT FAR.

The heat was still unbearable, we were in temperatures above 106 degrees and over, working well over sixty three hours per week, and extra watches besides. Having a good time, yes, but would be having a better time out of it. The evenings were comfortable and lit by brilliant moonlight. There was a heavy swell and the ship appeared to be shouldering its way into the wind and see-sawing visibly. I was still sleeping on the weather deck but on the 3rd March only a few of us slung there. I was awakened in the early hours by those who slept on camp beds beating a hurried retreat drenched through. The waves were just about lapping the underside of my hammock and I breathed a sigh of relief. So far, so good, but at 04.30 swoosh right over my head swept a vast amount of water. The wetting of my head was not too bad, but my hammock was filled, I was wet through, my clothes in the hammock nettles were soaked. As I sat up to adjust things another wave hit me. I lowered myself out of the sea-filled hammock into the water racing over the gunwhales. Standing there in my birthday suit with the wind blowing around and the sea water swirling through my legs knee deep I tried to lash up a drenched hammock, mattress and blanket and soaked clothes. I thought I might be swept overboard. I went below and dhobied my clothes and had a hot shower.

We went to Action Stations from 11.00 to 15.30 on the 4th March. At 17.00 we fell in for ceremonial entering of Fremantle, Western Australia. Again a low lying coastline, well wooded. Red roofed houses peeped from out the trees. On the jetty were ladies from Fremantle to welcome us and shower us with gifts. We each received a gift parcel containing: ½lb. chocolate, ¼lb. of sweets, notepaper and envelopes, a can of fruit, some plum pudding, and an undervest. Thanks were not enough to give to these volunteer ladies and the inhabitants of Fremantle.

I went ashore at 20.00 and made my way into the town. Within a few seconds of the docks you were in a delightful residential district. The streets were clean and well lit. We dined at a Chinese Restaurant, and had an excellent meal and fresh milk to drink. Which reminds me the ladies who welcomed us also provided gallons of fresh milk for us and wasn't it good! It was now late and we decided to go to a dance at the Town Hall, the Feast of the Lanterns Dance. The girls were very friendly and quite good dancers. There were few old time dances and some new to me, as Gypsy Tap. They had a progressive Barn Dance and the Pride of Erin. I had an excellent time, especially as the girl I was with was of Lancashire descent, her father came from Bootle. The people seem to have a cockney accent. Fremantle made me think how superior in cleanliness and layout it was compared with towns at home. Perhaps when the war is over emigration might be considered.

We put to sea on Sunday, 5th March and sailed through the Australian Bight. There was the warning of the possiblity of a cyclone. Certainly the seas were heavier and, of course, we were in the Roaring Forties. Two men off one of our escorting destroyers, the *Napier*, were washed overboard, and whether they were recovered or not I do not know. We had two long spells of practice Action Stations during the week. We passed through the Bass Straits on Friday, the 9th catching a glimpse of King's Island.

We arrived at Sydney on the 10th and berthed at 15.30. No one could miss the Bridge, even when well out. The entrance to the harbour was bleak, rugged sandstone cliffs falling down to the sea but, once passed, the hillsides were seen to be well wooded, they were covered with timber, reaching down to the creeks. Even in residential areas waves of trees swept round the houses. A school of porpoises pursued their rhythmic undulating course before us. Ferries criss-crossed over the harbour and trim yachts sailed by. As the great harbour opened up tall buildings broke the skyline and overshadowed the magnificent bridge. Sydney is vast, and as we drew near our berth we passed a delightful park. Smart cars were there in plenty. Strollers stopped and reclining couples in the park sat up and took an interest in us. We took an interest in them. The people at the swimming gala at the open air pool, just past the Sydney Rowing Club, stopped their activities and cheered us. We were berthed at Wooloomooloo which is flanked by the Botanic Gardens and the Domain. These open spaces adjoin docklands, and where else would you see such greenery so close to docks?

From here you could see the red sandstone cathedral of St. Mary, and Hyde Park. My shore run on Sunday consisted of walking across Sydney Bridge from which you can obtain wonderful views of the harbour and the surrounding suburbs. It is really a picturesque city. I made my way to the zoo at Tarranga. The open air zoo was crowded as well it might be. Not only is it well situated but imaginatively laid out. I particularly liked the koala bears and the kangaroos, emus, dingos and wallabies. We came back by ferry to Port Jackson and alighted at the foot of the bridge. I visited the Methodist Church in Castlereagh Street. Astounding! The evening service was held in the Lyceum, a modern theatre building, part of the Methodist complex, cream and beige decorated and concealed lighting. There would be about 2,000 in the congregation. The choir entered with measured tread. They wore purple cassocks and birettas. A battery of microphones surrounded the pulpit and choir. During the service a quartet and a soloist sang. Some of the congregation spoke to us, including a lady from Gorton, Manchester, and a gentleman from Leigh, Lancashire. Afterwards I walked around the streets and had supper at Everyman's Club and slept at the Naval House. On Monday there was another look around the streets, enquiries and a meal at the British Centre at Hyde Park, followed by dancing at the

Trocadero. This is the finest dance hall that I have ever seen. It is tastefully decorated, large, good floor, good dancers, and constantly changing fresh air. We met two sisters here, Pat and Irene O'Drane from Bondi and enjoyed their company. I'm doing well: shore leave again on Tuesday with an excellent meal at the St. Andrew's Hut (ice cream again) and then to see a film, "For Whom the Bells Tolls." Magnificent.

The ship's company was then given twenty three hours leave. In view of storing ship I had to take leave before the others. I decided to go to the Blue Mountains as I had been interested in them since reading about them as a small boy in school. I took the 13.08 from Exchange Station. It took a long time to leave the suburbs behind us. The plain was not very interesting but the climb into the Blue Mountains was most enjoyable. The valleys were smothered in trees. Here and there a small village would appear but most of them would be lost in the foliage. The stations were decked with hanging baskets. The only places I could remember of the places passed were Penrith and Bullaburra. After four hours I arrived at Katoomba. It had an altitude notice. As there was not much daylight left I hurried to the Jamieson Valley and Leura Falls. The view from Echo Point was breath taking. The tall trees which covered the valley looked like toys. I followed the Federal Path and looked down at the Falls but there was very little water coming down, nevertheless, you could imagine what the Cascades and the Bridal Veil Falls would look like. I was spell-bound and had to tear myself away from this magnificent scene in order to find accommodation.

I took another look at the Jamieson and when I reached the skirting road, I had been all alone for this time, I met an elderly gentleman who pointed out to me the Lion Rock and Emu Shadow. I hadn't time to look at the Three Sisters Rocks. This gentleman was on holiday and he directed me to one of the two places where I might find accommodation. He originally came from Scotland. At my third attempt to get sleeping quarters I was offered and accepted, for the place was overflowing with holiday makers, the share of a garden-shed-bedroom occupied by the hotel staff. I dined at the hotel and was the centre of attention. Royal Navy matelots were a rarity. An elderly gentleman approached me in the hotel lobby. He had emigrated from Newcastle, England, and he wanted to talk about the old country. He was very helpful and helped me to see other places of interest and whether the Falls were illuminated that night. He gave an informative tour of the town. He showed me the Kingsford Smith Memorial Park, a natural amphitheatre laid out in terraces and possessing an open air theatre, and flowering garden. A carillon was playing Christmas Carols. We stood yarning about England in the delicious cool of the evening. As we had been away for a good hour he made his way back to the Burlington suggesting where I might find amusement in Katoomba and, if I were not successful, to return to the Burlington and rejoin his group. A Canadian then stopped me and enquired if I were an Englishman requiring accommodation, as two girls were looking for me. I thought no more about this until I met the Scotsman again, this time accompanied by his wife. On returning to where he was staying he told his wife of our meeting. She immediately sent their two daughters in search of me as they had a spare room at the bungalow and that I would be most welcome to stay there and there would be no charge. It is amazing how caring people can be.

I danced at the Wentworth and had a smashing time, It wasn't my personality, I have none, but I was English and in a naval uniform, a very rare species. The Wentworth is a delightful little dance hall with an excellent floor. The holiday crowd was in good attendance and I did not lack for partners. There was no difficulty in joining a party where a charming blonde from Newcastle, N.S.W. did not give me the brush off. Another of the party, not as lovely as the blonde, was an exceptionally good dancer. Actually she was a dance teacher in Sydney and had won cups and medals

126

for dancing. We had supper of toasted sandwiches and delicious coffee before I took her back to the wooden chalet in the dell where she was staying.

I made my way back to the Burlington and slept fairly well and arose at 05.00. Katoomba was quiet but the town was sunlit at this hour and the mountain air was invigorating. The platform became crowded for the 06.30 train back to Sydney. I managed to get a seat and one of the bulky newspapers. Once more I enjoyed the mountain scenery and its timbered expanses. The journey back took only two hours and on entering Sydney joined up with the suburban traffic and crowded pullman cars. The rail gangs were hallooing all along the line and newspapers were flung from the trains to them. I breakfasted at the St. Andrew's C. of E. hut on a huge bowl of cereals and milk, a plate overflowing with bacon, two fried eggs and chips, bread and butter and jam, and coffee; all for the cost of 10d. I congratulated the lady helper who apologised that the bacon was not up to the usual standard. It was delicious.

On Saturday I took a working party to Randwick and Leichart. On the return journey the party persuaded me to let them have a bevy at a pub. This was dangerous for me, we might be seen, so I stayed on the lorry to guard the stores. I had, however, to drag them out of the pub after they had been there over half an hour. Luckily we were not spotted by passing Navy personnel. On Sunday I went over to Manley. Here is a huge swimming pool with its shark protection screen. Just over the hill you come to Ocean Beach which is the prettiest place I've seen. It possesses marvellous sands, a not too noticeable promenade with lawns and tall fir trees. Here and there is good surf bathing. St. Patrick's College, a very handsome building, stands on one headland whilst the Queenscliff Lifesaving Patrol Headquarters is at the other end of the bay, and just before you come to Curl-curl. Many cars were parked under the trees and picnic parties enjoyed themselves on the green sward. If England possessed a bathing place as picturesque and clean as Manley it would monopolise all holiday resorts.

I left Manley regretfully and went to the Methodist Church Club which is run on the same lines as the one at Belfast. Those in the Services had to stand and announce their name and home town. Most were Australians but the few British received tumultuous applause. Afterwards I was sought by the leader of the club, he came from Bedfordshire and his wife came from Urmston, Manchester. We had a long conversation about England and I had to accept an invitation to dinner at their house during the week. This I could not keep as we sailed on Wednesday at 15.15 and came back into Port Jackson at 12.00 on the 24th March and after a hectic storing period left again at 18.00.

We were informed that our next stop would be Manus one of the Admiralty Islands, off New Guinea, and after a short stay there we would proceed to the Philippines where General Macarthur was. I contracted tonsilitis, the old trouble, and went into Sick-bay where I was kept in bed until Good Friday when we arrived at Manus. I missed the scenic effect of this journey northwards through the Coral Sea, and the spurts past islands still in Japanese hands. The Admiralty Islands enclose a circular bay, some islands are more or less a mere strip of land containing a single row of palm trees, others were large and covered with vegetation. We put to sea on Saturday and sailed for the Philippines. En route we passed over the Embden Deeps, the deepest part of any ocean, being deeper than Mount Everest is high.

We arrived at Leyte on the 4th April. This appeared to be a number of small islands behind a larger one, possessing high mountains.

I went ashore on the 8th April. The sea was as calm as a pan of milk. The sun beat down on us making the hour and a half journey ashore very uncomfortable. We landed at St. Antoni's Beach, Samar. This is a small sandy stretch clustered with palm trees. Among the trees were large bamboo structures supporting a roof of plaited leaves and having open sides. A boxing tournament was in progress sponsored by the Americans. The structures had nameplates such as Yankee Stadium, and others recalled hotels and sporting arenas in the U.S.A. Away from the beach was a mound on which a huge crowd was milling. Here the Philippinos were selling local articles. The goods were not very attractive, but very dear. There were raffia sandals, plaited fibre coolie hats, knives in bamboo sheaths, raffia mats decorated with the words Philippines or Samar, handbags made of beads, eggs, hens and coloured birds. Many of the Yanks were bartering clothes, underwear, soap and practically everything you could think of including mosquito nets. A pair of wooden sandals cost 15 dollars. In the shallow waters where many Yanks were bathing a couple were practising sodomy. Men without women.

Leyte had not long been taken from the Japanese and we were told that all the women on the island had been raped and that V.D. was rife.

The journey back was in choppy water. In addition we had to tow the other liberty boat and this lengthened the trip. I was in the bows and was continually feeling the spray. I was drenched through and thankfully two hours later the *Formidable* hove in view.

Vice Admiral Vian came on board for an hour on the 9th. Later in the day we changed berth. At Divisions on the 9th the Skipper informed us that the *Indefatigable* had been hit by suicide Zeros and that twenty had been killed. The *Victorious* had had a near miss but the battle was going in our favour. The news broadcast announced that the *K.G.V.* had been hit and we learned that the *Tyne* and *Pennsylvania* had been damaged.

We sailed on Tuesday far too close to Japanese controlled bases. News came through on Friday, the 13th, that President F. D. Roosevelt of the U.S.A. had died. He had died the previous day. A Memorial Service was held on the Flight Deck at 15.10. We had been stationary for a day or two, oiling at sea, and waiting for the fleet so a full service of all except duty ratings was possible. The American complement on board were in full tropical rig. We commenced with the hymn: 'Abide with me', and followed by a few words by the padre of the help and inspiration given by F.D.R. The 23rd Psalm followed, although completely boxed up the padre. We then sang: 'O God our help in ages past'. An American officer read especially well verses 1—7 of chapter XXI from Revelations. Prayers were said and we closed with: 'Alleluia, the strife is o'er, the battle won' to the tune Victory.

We joined the fleet during the night of 13/14 April. Whether true or not the story is told that we signalled: 'Good Morning are you the B.P.F.?' and the reply was, 'Yes, I thought you were an aircraft carrier.' My version is, 'Hello, this is the Marie Celeste.'

Admiral Sir Philip Vian flew on board on the 15th and spoke to the ship's company. After saying how glad he was to have the *Formidable* with the Fleet he remarked that some of them were on the ship during its notable operations in the Mediterranean. He told us what to expect from the Japanese suicide bombers, the Judy, Sally and Zeke. Everything depended on aircraft recognition because of the similarity of their planes to some of ours; and the short range weapons because of the Japanese custom to take cover in cloud and dive on the fleet thereby rendering void the 4.5s. He wished us success in the operation to take place on the 16th and 17th.

We went to Action Stations on the 16th very early. Our object was to render unserviceable airfields on some islands off Formosa. Although we had action commentaries during the whole of the day I could not follow the action. The Skipper spoke to us that night of the first day's action. He congratulated our pilots on the performance they had put up (we had lost one aircraft, however). He then read to us a signal from A.C.1 (Admiral Vian)—A very heavy air attack was delivered today on the ships supplying the army in Okinawa. Over 100 aircraft came down. The Americans shot down 62. All these Japanese aircraft came from the north. It can be assumed that the fact we kept the aerodrome under bombardment all day prevented Japanese aircaft coming from the south to attack our large attack on Okinawa. The aircraft ranging parties received especial praise upon the way they had worked. Another heavy day was promised on Tuesday.

Sure enough, we were at Action Stations without breakfast. We secured later, however, in the afternoon and were relaxed until matters came worse. We had another spell at 17.00. One of our planes was brought down during the day and a thrilling rescue was made by the Walrus of the *Victorious*. The air rescue crew picked up the pilot within a mile of the island from which the Japanese were firing rifle shots at them. It is said that the Japanese signalled us saying that all the craters we had made on their airfields had been filled in, that the airfields were serviceable and that we had better go home. The Skipper spoke to us again on the 17th. Bouquets were thrown to the pilots, aircrews, flight parties, armourers, hangar parties, etc. etc. for their excellence, despite the long and strenuous day's work. He then spoke of the Battle of Okinawa. He said that the new Premier of Japan had realised that the battle was the beginning of the end for them. If the Americans can hold this island and maintain it not only would it bring about the bombing of Japan itself, but the entrance to the Yangtse and Korea. This would mean the strangling of Japan's life blood running into her from China. The Battle of Okinawa was going ahead of time but it was not going without bloody fighting. In order to conquer Okinawa hundreds of ships of all kinds would have to maintain supplies and for that reason the Japanese were throwing in tremendous attacks against them.

131

A signal was received from A.C.1—180 enemy planes had attacked and the Americans had shot down 116. This was a typical day. You can imagine that this was not done without considerable losses, and severe fighting. At present our part of the battle has prevented planes attacking from the south. Our time will come we must be prepared for heavy and bloody fighting.

06.00 Action Stations, Friday, the 20th. Our target was once more the Sakishima Gunto group of islands and Myako islands. A signal was received from A.C.1 indicating that these three days were the finest three days operations he'd seen. One of the American officers on board spoke over the S.R.E. to us, stating that he'd spent three years on American 'flat tops' in these waters but the spirit and efficiency of the *Formidable* was amazing and he concurred with A.C.1's signal entirely.

We returned to Leyte on the 23rd April, St. George's Day. Although the padre holds services on practically all saints' days, he missed this one. At Leyte sleeping between decks became irksome.

We sailed on Labour Day, May 1st and heard that the hammer and sickle of the U.S.S.R. was flying from the Reichstag, Berlin. Good old Joe. Mussolini had been captured by patriots near Lake Como and killed. We heard on May 2nd that Hitler had died, and the following day that Goebbels had committed suicide. How's that for a hat trick!

May 4th was momentous and tragic for us. Attacks were to be made on the Sakishimo Gunto, especially Ishigaki and Myako. We closed at 05.15. The usual brief reports were made by our action commentator over the tannoy as to what was happening during the battle. Down in the Lower Steering Position where I was with Johnny Yea very little could be gathered. It is here where instructions are received by voice pipe from the bridge. The quarter master and his team obey the commands to change the ship's direction by manually turning the huge wheel. Bells clang, the work is hard. Many changes are taking place. The pace is furious. We are keeping the plot of the ship's course. We heard a frenzied shout from the commentator on the bridge, then a loud crashing sound. The ship shuddered and jumped. The quarter master challenged the bridge. No reply. We were now in total darkness, the electric lights had failed. We turned on the emergency lighting and our torches. Filthy air came flooding through the pantalouvres. We could smell petrol. We were battened down and had no connection from the deck above us. It was ages before communication with the bridge was restored. Were we glad to hear the voice of Jimmy the One, Lieutenant J. B. Frewen. He enquired and was told of our circumstances by the Q.M. His cool and conversational reply was, 'I'm still here, but for how long I don't know.' The commentator's voice was not heard again. That was comforting. I was glad we had a job to do which required concentration, even though you did not know or see what was happening above. Much later we learned that a Jap plane had dropped a bomb on the flight deck near the island. A fire ensued but was soon put out. A signal from A.C.1. read: 'Good show, *Formidable*.' We did not know that this was in reply to our signal that the fires were out and casualties were being dealt with. It had sounded callous. Shrapnel from the bomb penetrated through many decks.

Details of what had happened we learned much later. The plane did not escape but was shot down. The bomb cratered the deck despite the armour plating, and had riddled the island. Eight ratings had been killed instantaneously, and more than sixty were injured, many seriously. Additional casualty centres had to be improvised, even the W.O.'s Mess and the Ward Room Ante Room were pressed into service. The hangar curtain had been ripped down, the huge beam spreadeagled the hangar. Fire parties and others filled in the crater with cement and the hole in the hangar deck was covered over. The island was completely riddled and resembled a pepper pot. Shrapnel penetrated right into the engine room and through the ship's bottom. Aircraft were damaged beyond repair both on the flight deck and in the hangar. The dead were buried at sea. Some of the casualties were so seriously injured that little hope of their survival is expected. Perhaps it is a little compensation to say Jap planes were destroyed. A Hellcat received a similar fate from our guns.

A.C.1 signalled later in the day—First strike bombed Myako airfield and flack positions; second carried similar attacks on Ishigaki runways and hits were scored in both attacks. Most runways were unserviceable. Hellcats shot down Jap planes between 11.15 and 11.38. The carrier force was attacked by two flights and the *Formidable* received a direct hit. A bomb hit the *Indomitable* but bounced off without exploding. The planes doing the damage were shot down. Other Jap planes were destroyed by our fighters. The Skipper spoke to us that night and complimented the crew on the manner in which they had stood up to their baptism of fire. It was necessary, however, that we carry on and that we would be at action stations in the morning. We were at dawn but the day was fairly quiet. Dinner that night when we had been hit was Irish stew, somewhat unpalatable, and no criticism of the galley, they too were at action stations. Much of the stew was ditched. The point I am making is that I passed through the Ward Room flat that evening while on ordinary duty and read the menu on the Ward Room Notice Board. There was a choice of nineteen dishes. I counted them.

We were at Action Stations on the 8th. Apparently the routine was to attack and withdraw for re-fuelling. During the re-fuelling an American Squadron attacked and thus constant attention was being paid to the Sakishima Gunto.

We heard over the radio that the war in Europe was ended at 02.40 French time, today, and that public holidays today and tomorrow were being held in the U.K. The news came from the American Broadcasting system in Okinawa but reception was poor. We picked out that crowds were gathering in Piccadilly Circus. The Day had arrived, we were in operation, but let's all celebrate as best we can.

Another of the injured died today and was buried at sea. Others injured have been taken on the Wessex. Two more have died. What a tragedy for their relatives who, on hearing of the end of the war in Europe, now hear of the death of their sons and husbands.

A signal was received yesterday that seven allied ships were sunk and thirty damaged off Okinawa by the Japs.

Wednesday, the 9th. Celebrations at home and I would be celebrating with you, but it is ironical that we are still in action. At 18.00 a Kamikaze (Divine Wind) Jap plane made a suicidal attack on us. We were fortunate in some ways as although the bridge was peppered and flames licked all around, only one rating was killed, and four injured. The flight deck was dented again, sets riddled with shrapnel, aircraft became a complete write-off, and there was danger of fire spreading to the hangar. Another attacking plane was shot down before it could crash on the deck. The pilot's body from the Kamikaze was found forward and ditched. The *Victorious* was also hit. *Uganda* signalled: 'Deepest Admiration'. That night the Skipper spoke to us, just a few words, but they were resonant with sincerity. 'I've cursed you. I've pushed you around, but my God, I admire you. I've never had a better ship's company and never will have one as good. We're going now to the fuelling areas to lick our wounds. Good night.' The 'Goodnight' was something, previously all he had ended with was, 'That's all.'

10th May. The injured were later taken off the ship by cradle to one of the destroyers. The Bridge, blackened by fire and bristling with wedges which filled the holes, was painted over. The Kamikaze pilots I learned have a wire noose round their neck which immediately decapitates them on crashing: hence the pilot's torso was up forward and the severed head, which was waved about, somewhere else. The usual attacks on the Sakishima Gunto were made on the 12th and 13th, but we did not have the assiduous attention paid to us this time, possibly perhaps because we were attacking from a more easterly position. Our efforts

135

were successful. Strips were rendered Uncle Sugar, transport assemblies were hit, etc.

Respite once more in the fuelling grounds, but hellishly sticky below. On the 15th, the first commissioning anniversary was celebrated, rather the anniversary of the arrival on board of the big draft. We had cake and fruit for tea, and a Dance Band on the flight deck during the first dog. Subby Grassam, dressed as a baby and draped in a diaper and well talced, was wheeled on a bogy by Lofty Holland in nursemaid's uniform, a supposedly prim nursemaid, and you cannot get primmer than Lofty Holland. A two tier cake was towed on a dodgem, the cake was on a tea wagon over which a cook hovered as a flunky. So on the eve of action we made merry. What happened on the Eve of Waterloo? There was a sound of revelry by night. Action on the 16th was quiet. We returned once more to the fuelling grounds, presumably for a breather, although these periods are work periods busily spent in storing and transferring stores.

Although comparatively out of danger we were confronted by a worse danger. Fire at sea. It happened in this way: an armourer was attending to the guns on an aircraft in the hangar and they actually fired. Soon the hangar was ablaze. The wonderful efficiency of the ship was soon in operation, but with high octane fuel and bombs close by the scene, the hazards were high, and so nearly were we. The sprinklers went into action and the fire parties slaved away. Aircraft were revved up and in this way the fire was confined to a certain area. We were five minutes off 'Abandon ship' and this order was in operation with crew assembled at their various stations. Cruisers and destroyers sailed in to rescue us if need be. I, however, knew nothing about this. I was working deep down in the ship alone where pipes did not reach. I began to make my way back to the mess for a meal and found every hatch more than difficult to open. They had been tightly secured. Each deck I came to was deserted. An eerie feeling. On arriving at hangar level the trailing hoses and the smell of fire were definitely in evidence. But the panic was over and the fire was under control.

We heard details of the demobbing of groups 1—11. This cheered us. There was an unconfirmed report from Reuter of the Peace Proposals by Japan, which proposals were not accepted as they were unconditional.

Sunday, May 20th. Whitsunday. Peace in Europe. We were at Action Stations again. The morning was foggy and this delayed the strikes. The *Quilliam* ran into the *Indomitable* during the fog but, so far as is known, not much damage was done. The Yanks asked us to turn on the heat but in view of all our troubles, fire and foe, we could not put up much cover as C.A.P. After the usual length of attacks we returned to the fuelling area en route for Sydney. We arrived at Leyte on Thursday, 24th, staying a few hours only. New Guinea was on our starboard on the 27th.

During the week I heard on the radio that groups 1—11 were to be demobbed by the end of August, and 750,000 would be out of the forces by the end of the year. Naturally I spread the news and many were soon calling at their local pub, wearing civvy suits, etc. There appeared to be a suppression of the news. The news I heard was at 2 am. B.B.C. programmes and Australian also, were not heard on the S.R.E. only the Okinawa broadcast and this despite Churchill's speech having been relayed to us. There was a technical difficulty. The next news we heard was about disarming the German Navy, and in the Far East. Consequently we could not hope for demobilisation at the same rate as the Army and the R.A.F. Releases would lag behind at first and, perhaps later, might overtake the other Services. This signal caused much bitterness and was regarded as a Betrayal of the Navy. We wrote home to this effect. Shortly afterwards a further signal came through somewhat easing the situation.

We fell in for entering Sydney Harbour on Friday, 1st June. It was colder and slight mists obscured the view.

Planes hid the damage on the flight deck, whilst paint obliterated the damaged state of the Bridge. We were looking forward to shore leave but it was sparse. Even make-and-mends on Saturdays and Sundays disappeared. Work was unending and shore leave commenced at 19.00 which was constricting. Peter Hibbert, a late member of the mess, came on board from the *Pioneer*. We talked of old times. Runs ashore meant a visit to the flicks or lazing on the nearby Domain on Sunday if a make-and-mend had been given. The motor dinghies of the rich dodged between the ferry boats that afternoon, trains seemed to crawl across the Sydney Harbour Bridge, and ships lay at anchor below us. One Sunday we made our way to the Botanical Gardens into Macquarie Street. We passed the Conservatorium of Music which was originally horse stables.

We were granted four days leave, very acceptable, of course, but after nine months not very good, especially considering what the shore based ratings enjoyed. The hospitality of the Australians is amazing. You could enquire at the British Centre at Hyde Park, a wonderful building erected and paid for in no time by the Australians with restaurant, dormitories, dance floor, rest rooms, enquiry desk, you name it they had it, hostesses, and holidays with Australian people. We enquired about going to a sheep station. Unfortunately the rains came, day after day of sweeping rains. Reports were coming through of floods up north, of delayed train services, and towns nearly submerged. The sheep station was out. Bob Jamison on returning from leave invited Alan and me to go and stay with his uncle and aunt. We told the British Centre who cancelled our previous request and telegraphed the Sutherlands to say we were coming.

During the intervening period I attended the Southern Cross Hut, a Communist Centre, and enjoyed a social evening there. Many Australian ratings were there, men and women, all of them party members. On the *Shropshire* I was told seventeen members met regularly in the Chart House and discussed their political beliefs. In the Army

138

they took an active part in the educational discussions. Most of them sported C.P. badges. The evening was spent in dancing, a sketch about the leaders of the political parties having a private discussion on the efforts to suppress the working class and what they would say in public about their benefactions. There was an extremely good piano recital by a lad about ten years of age. I was invited to and accepted an invitation to the Miles home in North Sydney. Mr. Miles is the local secretary of the C.P. His house was wooden and nicely furnished. A red cushion embroidered with a yellow hammer and sickle was on a settee and a picture of Lenin on the wall. The family had emigrated from County Durham, at first to Brisbane. They told me of the depression years and the hardships of that period. These were grim times, yet they enlivened it with humour and subterfuges, e.g. some of them would register in fictitious names and doubled up on the dole. He talked about the working conditions in Australia and state enterprises.

On other leaves I saw the comedy 'Kiss and Tell'; an excellent play 'Voice of the Turtle'; and a variety show, definitely blue and which would never have been allowed in England, called 'Greet the Fleet'.

June 16th. At last the day for our leave arrived. Alan and I dined at the Anzac Club before entraining at Central Station for Corrimal on the South Coast of N.S.W. Some others from the *Formidable* were also travelling down there and we joined up with Vincent and Pogson. A youngster of four years of age kept us amused. He had the cheeriest smile, no trace of shyness yet he was not precocious. He sang songs and talked incessantly to some Australian soldiers who doubled up in laughter.

From the carriage windows we caught glimpses of sandy beaches and heavy rollers. A good augury for our four days. It was an exceptionally pretty coast. A colliery was seen at Scarborough, a very different scene from our colliery towns. We arrived at Corrimal in the half light. George, a son of our hosts, met us. He made pleasant conversation on our way to his home in Midgley Street. The roads were none too good generally flanked by ditches over which you leaped to gain a footpath which would be a single line of flagstones, or none at all. The homes were all wooden bungalows no uniformity of their design or sites. George knew everyone in the village as there were constant 'Goodnights' to us. Noises made by frogs sounded like rattles filled the night air, but I never saw one although I looked carefully. A few stray horses cropped grass in the streets.

The Sutherlands were at the wicket gate to greet us: Mr. and Mrs. Sutherland, their daughter Jane and her husband Billy. The Sutherlands came from Scotland in 1910 and still retain a Scots accent. Mr. Sutherland is small and wiry and a miner. Mrs. Sutherland is plump and pleasant. We were very much at home the moment we met them. Their bungalow is called 'Carriden' their home town near Bo'ness. The house had the usual corrugated steel roof, an open verandah stretching across the front of the house. There was a wide lobby with bedrooms on either side. Then there was another bedroom and the dining room. The rooms at the back were a living room and scullery. A coke stove heated the dining room and the back of it heated the kitchen range. On the painted wooden walls were photographs of the family. A settee and chairs, a large walnut table and sideboard were also items of furniture. Our bedroom contained a single and double bed, compactum, dressing table and wash-hand stand. A window opened on to the verandah.

A marvellous meal awaited us; Mrs. Sutherland is a wonderful cook. Our feet were well under the table. I was home again. After tea George took us to the pictures. On the way we called for his young lady, Gwen, a charming girl with blonde hair. Her mother came from Worcestershire and her father was a Dane. The following morning we were able to see what Corrimal was like. It nestles between the Australian Divide, which is well wooded, and the sandy coast. To the rear of the house towers Broken Nose Hill.

140

Corrimal reminded me of the pictures depicting the pioneer places of America. The houses ranged from the simple early type, which had no more design than a box, and modern ones with horizontal windows and smart patios. We set off after breakfast with the idea of climbing Broken Nose Hill, but stayed at Mr. Henson's bungalow for the whole morning. The Hensons came from the Nottinghamshire/Derbyshire border. Mr. Henson started off as a miner but now he was the proprietor of a bus company. As he had paid cash down for his last Leyland bus he had done quite well. He was most enthusiastic about England and he had enjoyed a six months' visit to the Old Country in 1938.

We saw Woonoona play Corrimal during the afternoon at Rugby League, surely a reminder that most of these people came from Lancashire and Yorkshire. Sunday games were confined to Rugby League and Saturdays were given over to soccer. In passing George and his elder brother Gerry are star turns at most sport and fifteen cups they had won fill the sideboard at Carriden. After a super tea we sat round the fire and yarned for an hour or so. They showed us photographs of their first home in Australia. Mr. Sutherland first settled in Lithgow in the Blue Mountains. He built his house with planks of wood nailed together and fastened to the lee of a cliff face. These people were indeed pioneers and if they had said that they had travelled in covered wagons I would have believed them. They said many Lancashire people lived there and, on looking at photographs of their second home which was named Daisy Nook, which is near to where I live, they remembered that they took it over from a Mrs. Bardsley from Manchester.

Mr. Sutherland took us to the St. Andrew's Presbyterian Church at night. This is not a cathedral but a pretty wooden church, with a good preacher and a small congregation. Monday, the 18th, was celebrated as the King's Birthday and consequently was a holiday. Gerry was representing the South Coast in a soccer match in Sydney and most of the family were going down to the match. Mr. Sutherland took us to Kiama.

We travelled by bus to Woolongong and thence to Kiama passing on the way Illawarra Lakes. These are not strictly lakes, being sea filled. The wide expanse of water, tree fringed and reflecting the blue sky and the mountains, were reminiscent of the English Lake District.

Kiama is a lovely little seaside resort, its main attraction being the Cathedral Rocks and the Blow Hole. The latter is a cleft in the rocks through which the sea rushes and throws up a jet of water hundreds of feet high in rough weather. As we were visiting on a beautiful day the jet was only sixty feet high. We caught the bus back to Woolongong passing through Port Kembla which had been built on swamp land, and Steeltown where Lysachts and the Commonwealth Rolling Mills are. A ship was stranded on the rocky coast, still unbroken after a year or so.

That night we danced at the Masonic Hall at Bulli. We had quite a good time at the invitation and expense of the local Patriotic Committee. I danced the evening with Caroline who worked at Vickers the big woollen firm. She invited me in for supper but, as it was late, I did not want to keep the Sutherlands up and said that I would see her the following day. Unfortunately other arrangements had been made for me. One of our stokers told me that he was her companion the next night.

Tuesday, the 19th. Mr. Henson had lent his bus gratis to the Bulli Committee to take the British lads up to the Bulli Pass and he called for us to go. We had heard a lot about the Pass and the many accidents there, some fatal. The day was glorious and the bus climbed slowly up the Pass to Panorama Look-out. From here you could see far down the coast to Jervis Bay. Illawarra Lakes shimmered in the distance and smoke from Port Kembla soon cleared up to reveal the five islands. The coast contained many sandy beaches, you could hardly believe that this was a coal mining area. The plain was lacerated by creeks. Trees on the Great Divide swept down to the Pacific. From the woods

142

small communities peeped. The railway train looked like a toy Hornby engine crawling along, whilst the circular reservoir reminded me of the static water tanks in war time Britain. Another good viewpoint was Sublime Lookout and from here you could see Scarborough, N.S.W.

There were many different kinds of trees: fern, gum and cabbage trees. At this time of the year the red flowers of the coral trees blazed trails among the greenery. The lantaman hedges and the warrantah are particularly lovely.

The seaside resort of Austinmer lay to our left with the joint villages of Bulli-Woonoona before us, and Corrimal to the right. Tarrawarra was on the slopes of the Divide.

Mr. Burrows, the President of the local Patriotic Fund was our guide and he pointed out the various landmarks. He kept us alive with stories of the early settlers. He had come out over fifty years ago and was of Irish descent. In telling three of his stories try and imagine a stockily built man with grey hair, a reddish face and laughing eyes, and with the gift of the blarney. The stories are true and reveal the shrewdness of the early settler.

In the early days of immigration each person had to show that he had £100. Pat would arrive and he was to see that this was the right place for others of his family. On the family's arrival Pat would meet them on their arrival in Sydney. He would lend £100 to one of his family and get him into Australia. He would lend the same £100 to another member of the family, and so on. Mr. Burrows maintained that there were in Bulli alone a hundred and more immigrants with £100 between the lot of them.

O'Brien's bull, Terence, was killed by his neighbour's bull so O'Brien pointed out that compensation was required. The neighbour's offer was not satisfactory so they decided to approach Andy, a Scot, who had legal aspirations. Andy settled the case and told O'Brien that his fee would be two guineas. O'Brien paid up muttering, 'God preserve me from my friends.'

O'Brien was a butcher and when Andy's dog stole a leg of mutton off the counter he decided to get his own back on

Andy. He asked Andy what redress he had against a person whose dog had stolen something. Andy replied that he was entitled to compensation. O'Brien joyfully explained that Andy owed him two shillings, the value of the meat stolen, as it was Andy's dog which was the thief. Andy paid up and then charged O'Brien 10/6d for legal advice.

There was an election for the council and after the result was declared the successful candidate got uproariously drunk. His agent persuaded him to say a few words to the crowd waiting outside the hotel and thank them for the support they had given him. He did so in these words. 'For the last three weeks I have been kissing your arses, now you can kiss mine for the next three years!'

Mr. Burrows also told us of the brigs which were put to sea out of Port Kembla because of the high seas and the danger of their being sunk in the harbour. Both brigs and the crews were lost.

Standing on Sublime Lookout and listening to these stories was most enjoyable.

We went to Woolongong in the afternoon, called for Gwen at the shop where she worked and took her to lunch. After that we shopped. Our shopping was at the Flinders Hotel where we met with a crowd of stokers from our ship. The school numbered twelve and it was everlasting drinks. At last we got away and started to shop. We reached one shop but had to return as we wanted to relieve ourselves. Australian towns apparently do not go in for public conveniences, at least you cannot find one when it is needed. So back to the Flinders, more drinks as the school was still there, out into the street to shop, arrive at the same shop but had to make a hurried return to the Flinders. I think we would still be there on this routine but the hotel had to close sometime.

We went to the pictures in Woolongong at night, the cinema in Corrimal did not open on Tuesdays. As the last bus back left early we had to have a taxi home.

I have not mentioned that there is no sewerage in Corrimal, nor for that matter in the other villages. We used

144

a privy at the bottom of the garden. Each house had a privy and all of them looked like sentry boxes. The point I wish to make is that overhanging the privy was a lemon tree weighed down with luscious fruit.

We left Corrimal on Wednesday morning. Mr. Henson's bus took us to Bulli Station, gratis, and so ended a perfect holiday.

I should have mentioned that at the dance which was held for us the last waltz was danced to a lovely tune. It was a Maori song, the words were easily learned as the local folk sang it. The song was, 'Now is the hour' which became very popular much later in Britain.

Back to work. Perhaps those four days are still with me and making us all realise what we are missing.

On Sunday the 24th visitors were permitted over the ship and Jack brought along the families who had befriended him. Crowds thronged over the Domain and through the dockyard gates. My Corrimal friends were too far away so I helped Chief Johns out by accompanying his lady's friend over the ship. She was Mary Wynn a most charming girl. The afternoon was delightful so after going over the ship we had supper in town. Mary is a singer and does a fair amount of work for the A.B.C. She is also a party member. Unfortunately she had an engagement with a friend, a University professor, later at a musical society.

I went to the Methodist Mission in Castlereagh Street. It was overflowing, so that some of the congregation had to sit in the aisles, on the stairs, and over one hundred stood at the back. What wonderful congregations this church gets.

I stayed for the Social Hour after the Service. The Rev. Piggott, the padre at Royal Arthur, was there, and I had quite a good chat with him. He related a story of Naval diplomacy. A young O.D. was in Chatham Naval Hospital and called the Matron, Sister. She replied icily that she was not Sister, but Matron. The O.D. added brightly, 'But you look young enough to be my sister.'

We sailed on the 27th June and arrived at the Admiralty Isles on the 4th July. After a short stay brimming with storing, we left on the 6th July. On the 12th the Skipper spoke to us—'The last time I spoke to you was at Gibraltar. Now that the war in Europe is over many of you are thinking of home and how soon this war will be over. No doubt many of you are wondering why we are out here. It is good for us to realise the reason and the necessity for being here, but there are many Japanese, the estimate is roughly 90,000,000. In the last sixty years they have studied and learned all there is to know in the industrial world, power and machines. Their outlook is different from ours and their humanity is 300 years behind us, also their kindness and love. In six years they have got control of cheap labour. With great arms and ruthlessness they would have gone overland and taken China, Australia, New Zealand, Canada, India and even U.S.A. and no power would have stopped them if they had sufficient time. Eventually they would have taken us. Thus, this war so far from our homes is for our preservation and not for profits and commercial markets. After the present period of operation the plan is to return straight to Sydney, unless something prevents this. We will be part of the American Fleet, actually manoeuvering with them, although their ships will be out of sight over the horizon. The operation is planned with the B.29 bombers. These bombs can destroy factories and industrial plants and set fire to industrial areas better than we can, but small and important raids can be made by carriers. 180 aircraft have been damaged in the last 6—10 strikes without any ship being attacked. This does not mean that we shall not be attacked later. Every man and officer during the next three days should ask himself, "Do I know exactly what my job is, and do I understand my gear?" There is still time in the next three days to learn and know what is required of us. Good luck and good hunting to our aircrews.'

We heard during the next few days of a typhoon which had struck the American Fleet in early June. The bows of the *Pittsburgh* had been blown off and there was danger of her stern suffering a similar fate. About twenty three ships had been damaged. Luckily we missed it. The weather was much colder and the seas heavier; the former to our relief.

An icecream machine which had been installed at Sydney was now working and although it had broken there was a chance of obtaining some every fourth day. On the 12th July I had my first taste of it. Delicious.

Meanwhile the Americans had commenced heavy carrier raids on Tokyo and contrary to all naval precedent not only announced that the raids were taking place but the names of the ships taking part. Tuesday, 17th July, saw us up at 03.00 at Action Stations. Forces of the U.S.A. 3rd Fleet, augmented by our carriers, launched an attack in great strength against targets in Tokyo area. Admiral W. F. Halsey, U.S.A. was in command of the combined forces. Vice Admiral Sir Bertram Rawlings and Vice Admiral Sir Philip Vian were in technical command of the British Task Forces and Carriers respectively. In our Force were the *Formidable, Victorious, Implacable* and *K.G.V.*, *Newfoundland, Black Prince* and others. We caught sight of the American Fleet during one part of the day. On the whole the day was uneventful. Our strikes got off but little or no opposition was encountered. Perhaps the most important part of the day was that the radio was permitted to name us as taking part, and San Francisco enlarged upon this item. Our attack was directed principally against Honshu and the industrial area of Hitachi. The battlewagons were close inshore at night and heavily bombarded the area north of Tokyo. It was estimated that from 25 miles north of Tokyo to Hitachi which is about 75 miles north of Tokyo, was a sheet of flames and an area of explosions. We retired to our fuelling area on the 19th. Meanwhile we were expecting the typhoon to burst over us. Preparations were made accordingly: stores lashed down, hatches battened securely. The typhoon had struck Japan. Although the seas cut up rough, it wasn't that which scared us but submarines. I believe, however, that our depth charges

147

shook a Yankee submarine. On Tuesday, the 24th we struck at Tokyo although the weather was thick. Air strips and areas in southern Honshu were attacked, buildings strafed, radar installations shot up. A C.V.E. was located in the inland sea, and when last seen this carrier was down at the stern and its back broken. Three ships were seen unloading, one was definitely sunk and two damaged if not actually sunk. Other small ships were pranged. Planes were destroyed on the ground and three were shot down. Admiral Nimitz announced the attack when it was taking place.

Alarm-to-arms and Action Stations were the order of the day on the 25th. I managed a breather between 17.00 and 18.00 when I saw the American Fleet on the horizon. The end of the day was hectic. We were attacked by torpedo bombers, but our fighter groups, finally reduced to one plane, the others having run out of ammunition or fuel, scattered them after shooting down three. The Americans had stated that these planes were friendly and consequently put up no fighter cover. On hearing that we had shot them down they sent night fighters to engage the groups. There was a good number of planes in each group. We were undoubtedly saved by the vigilance and the courage of our pilots. News came through late at night that the Japanese Fleet had suffered heavily from the carrier plane attacks. Carriers, battleships, cruisers and destroyers all had been sunk. On Friday we oiled in readiness for our attacks the following day. Once more the inland sea and the shipping caught it besides shore installations, air strips and towns. The B.29s are making devastating raids and in addition to dropping leaflets the Americans are announcing to the enemy which towns were to be the next targets. Apparently the Japanese had asked what our peace proposals were and certainly over the radio our terms were broadcast.

During the fuelling periods we had P.T. on the flight deck. At times they were hilarious as the exceptionally strong winds made standing on the deck an acrobatic feat, never mind doing P.T. Many times as we flung our arms wide and high we thought we would become airborne. Sunday the 29th. We didn't strike but it wasn't a day of rest. We were informed of the following day's operations. Our attacks had been successful and unique. The Japanese had been completely cut off from troops and supplies on the mainland. All their shipping had been confined to the inland sea and was being slowly and systematically burned and destroyed. What was left of their fleet had been damaged, including four battleships and as many carriers and several destroyers. Several cruisers had certainly been eliminated. The Admiral of the Pacific Fleet had announced that what was left of the enemy fleet could be destroyed by an American destroyer force. That was not a tall statement. The unique show we had put up, and the fact that the Japanese had shown no opposition is very clear that the end is near. That did not mean that we could relax as they might change their minds and send out a large number of aircraft. Monday the 30th saw us striking again and once more to devastating effect. The 31st we oiled. The next few days were uneventful just trailing our coats. We cruised round near to the mainland and not until the 8th August did we propose to attack again.

On the 7th August we learned that there were such things as atomic bombs, their use and the reason for our not striking. Apparently scientists and universities in the U.K. had been working on the project of splitting the atom since the war began. America had co-operated and apparently we had just beaten the Germans to it. £500,000,000 had been spent on this one item and in New Mexico the final outcome was that the atom had been split. The steel tower on which it had been exploded was vaporised, men were blown off their feet five miles away and its effect was felt 250 miles away. These were the bombs being dropped by parachute on Japan, and hence our keeping out of the way. Admittedly visibility was not too good when we went into attack on the 8th and did not make a single strike. But it hadn't been for over a week, so that reason and the typhoon could not be for ever the reason of our not attacking. Further we did not have a C.A.P. and at times cruised at 10 knots. Perhaps the answer is the atomic bomb which was dropped by Super Fortresses. The Japs announced a meeting of their Cabinet this afternoon. Is the end near, possibly hours away?

August 8th. The Russians declare war on Japan. How opportunist can you get? I must revise my ideas on communism.

The next few days broadcasts on the ship were about the atomic bomb. At first we felt sick at the enormity of it, or was it that we did not understand? Hiroshima was the trial town and one bomb destroyed two-thirds of it. We went to attack on the 9th and hit shipping, aerodromes, docks, planes, trains, etc.

At 9 pm, on the 10th the B.B.C. news really hit us. We heard it on S.R.E. This in itself was an exceptional occurrence. 'Japan has agreed to the terms of surrender in accordance with the Potsdam Conference, except that Hirohito is to remain Emperor.' For a minute there was complete silence—then we shouted to each other across the messdeck. Then we sipped cups of tea in complete silence. What thoughts were running through our heads? We discussed the news until pipe-down. Except for that one minute there was no exuberance, but sheer thankfulness that the end had come.

We awaited more news of the end and in the meantime lashed everything down because of the possibilitry of another typhoon sweeping over us. We dared not relax because of treachery by the Japs. They might send suicide attacks upon us as a climax to the war.

A story is told that Admiral Sir Bruce Fraser signalled Sir Philip Vian that the end of hostilities might be announced within the next few days, and the reply was made: 'I hope that it does not interfere with my operation.'

150

B.29 and atomic raids were suspended and our attack arranged for the 12th was postponed. The naval attacks of the 9th and 10th had been more than successful, we appear to have hit everything. In view of the possible acceptance of unconditional surrender we did not strike. On the 12th we could see the Yankee Fleet and about a dozen oilers. Still no news of the end. Celebrations in Trafalgar Square and Piccadilly but on the 12th the Japs hit an American capital ship at Okinawa. The fleet split up on the 12th and we proceeded south. Again we were on the fringe of a typhoon. The waves had beards and the long swell of the Pacific shouldered us relentlessly. We listened to the news on the 13th but the Japs are still silent. We hear that the fleet has attacked the mainland again. Buzzes galore circulate. If peace comes then the fleet will split up. Part of it will lie off Japan and the other part will be required for occupational work. That is definite.

During the lulls of oiling we got a chance of promenading on the flight deck and watched flying fish and dolphins playing follow my leader. That was our only amusement. How the end drags! The silent Jap, the unbearable heat, the monotonous food, the same radio version of James Burns' reply to the Japs churned our incessantly, rapid Russian advances, Navy hits again, Chinese gains, resistance in Burma, celebrations at home. Oh! it's a lovely war.

Perhaps one or two signals will illustrate our value: C-in-C. Adv. H.Q. signalled: 'To the extent that you have eliminated naval vessels, aircraft and shipping you have simplified our problem for the future. Well done and continued good hunting.' Com. 3rd Fleet said: 'To Dumbbes and Lifeguard, to CAP and men of surface teams, to the valiant British Force on the right flank, well done. For the Flying Fighters who fought it out over Japan—to a smashing victory. I have no words but those which can add to the glory of the factual records they wrote with their courage, their blood, and their lives.' A.C.1 on the 10th said to the aircraft carrier squadron, 'Two great days in which all have manfully played their part in making

151

the enemy stagger. And a living standard has been set for two days of operation from our carriers.' VABPF signalled: 'On parting company I can speak for the whole Fleet in saying how much we have admired the gallantry and persistence of the aircrews and the stout-hearted work of the carriers. You have written a chapter in Naval Flying which has been rewarded by helping to write finish to Japan and her Fleet. No less valuable for our future are the links you have helped to forge between us and the U.S. Fleets.' U.S. Task Force 38 send to VABPF a message: 'It is fitting our great allies on many a previous hard fought battle should have helped in the last campaign. Good fortune to those who are departing and my humble respect to all of your gallant pilots.'

We expected news of unconditional surrender at 21.00 on the 14th August, but we did not hear it. During the day I saw spouting of a whale and a few more flying fish. It was cool on the weather deck at night. The low hum of the engines and the higher swishing sound of the waves, stars agleam and shooting stars arcing, a moon silvering the sea, the dark silhouettes of accompanying ships, all made a peaceful scene.

We went to duties on the 15th and at 08.35 a pipe was made that the Prime Minister would speak at 09.00 and a stand-easy would be given. Needless to say we had our ears glued to the S.R.E. speaker at this time and, although we did not hear Clem Atlee, we got an American Station giving the news of the end. We got a make-and-mend in the afternoon and spliced the mainbrace.

The 16th was an unusual routine. Charley 07.00, breakfast 07.35, P.T. 08.20, change to white tropical rig immediately afterwards and clear lower deck at 08.50 when V.A. Sir Philip Vian would speak to us on the flight deck. We could not hear a word from this unsmiling faced fellow; the wind was tearing around us and deadening his speech. Apparently we might be going back to Sydney for a short spell; a fleet was on its way for occupational and operations work, and we would follow later. There would be a lot of work to do and we must not bank on getting out soon. The Skipper would be leaving us. That was about all we could gather from dozens of ratings standing near the mike, and that's about all they heard. We then had a stand-easy and then fell in again on the flight deck for a Thanksgiving Service. This closed in a storm drenching us. We turned to at 10.30 and had another make-and-mend. We arrived at the Admiralty Islands on the 18th and sailed for Sydney on the 19th. After Divisions this day the Skipper spoke to us at great length; his theme was spreading good will between Great Britain, U.S.A. and the U.S.S.R. in order to preserve peace in our time. He told that there was the possibility of our going to Hong Kong.

We arrived at Sydney on the 23rd. The morning was hazy as we steamed into the harbour. Aircraft zoomed above us and dipped overhead. Crowds had gathered on the headlands waving and cheering. At Watson's Bay, Mrs. Macquarie's Chair in the Outer Domain, and on Cremona Point parties were welcoming us. We entered first followed by *Implacable* with the destroyers *Grenville, Urchin* and *Undine*. The *Victorious* with the *Urania* entered later.

I went ashore that night with Alan Hislam to dine at le Coq d'Or, a restaurant we liked. The hierarchy had tried to have it put out of bounds for us lesser beings, but the Australians thought that our money was as good as our betters. Two subbies from our ship stared somewhat disdainfully at us. I did not notice two officers enter the restaurant, I was too busy enjoying the meal, when one of the officers approached our table. He was Lieutenant Commander Frank Hawley who attended the same chapel as I do in Newton Heath. We exchanged gossip from back home. The icy stare of our near diners changed. Frank was on the *Implacable* which had tied up astern of us at Wooloomooloo that afternoon. He invited us over for a drink the following day. This was a remarkable thing to do from one upper deck to the lower deck. Unfortunately the invitation could not be honoured as they flashed up and sailed the following morning. We had another run ashore on Sunday and visited the Koala Sanctuary at Pennant Hills outside Sydney. There were only a few of these animals there but we could touch them as they slept in the gum trees. All they seemed to do was sleep in peculiar positions leaning on one ear, then wake up to nibble a few leaves from the gum trees. There were emus and kangaroos and an aborigine was throwing boomerangs in the park.

We couldn't get into the Methodist church that night, it was full, so to show our wide interests we went to the Independent Theatre to see 'They came to a City'. The next week was occupied with storing. I went to the Minerva, a lovely theatre, to see 'Love in Idleness', and had a blind date another day, not too good.

On Saturday, 1st September I watched Balrain v. Eastern Suburbs in the R.L. League Final on Sydney Cricket Ground. The accommodation in the stand was terrific, but I was disappointed with the size of the ground. That night C.P.O. Johns and I took Mary and Daphne to the Town Hall where a concert version of Carmen was being given. Mary was in the orchestra. Afterwards we had supper. Sunday we were still storing. In the afternoon I did a duty guide tour of the ship escorting seven people. Alf Leeming later on came aboard so the three went ashore to fix up leave.

The British Centre fixed us up at Gosford. We left the ship at noon on the 3rd September. Gosford is on the Hawkesbury River and is the market town for the orange and citrus fruit growing countryside. We passed through well wooded country, crossed the Hawkesbury River a few times, now and again catching glimpses of the river reflecting perfectly a blue sky and fringes of pines and gum trees. It was dark when we alighted at the wooden railway station. A British Centre lady met us and packed us into a taxi. We were to stay with Mr. and Mrs. Higgs, Hazeldawn, Frederick Street. Their large bungalow was well furnished but our sleeping arrangements were somewhat cramped.

We improvised the arrangements and really enjoyed the invitation to stay with our hosts. Later that night Ron Biggs a stoker from the *Victorious* arrived and a single bed was set up for him.

Mr. Higgs was the foreman of the neighbouring quarry; his son, a lad of 15, was the fireman there. Mrs. Higgs is small and a lively character. Her activities in the past will give you an idea of her personality: horse riding, parachute jumping and driving a car recklessly. Marjorie, her daughter and her friend Dawn did the housework. We had a better chance of doing the rounds and looking over the place the following morning. The bungalow had a verandah on three sides which we decided to use for sleeping. The big garden contains many orange bushes and we used to pluck an orange before breakfast. A few hens were kept and a cockatoo. Skipper, a smooth haired terrier, attached itself to us.

Gosford is not big but it is pretty. The valley is wide and here the Brisbane Water spreads itself out. The Sydney end of the valley appears to be blocked by the Lion Rock, making it look like a huge lake surrounded by hills. We entered the Union Hotel at 2 pm and stayed until closing time, 6 pm.Licensing hours are very peculiar—beer would go off sale and come on again later. Consequently the intervals were spent in consuming Aussie whisky, etc. Strange, I was still sober at the end of the session. We dined at the canteen before proceeding to Mattock's Dance Hall. The four of us at the Higgs called on Ron's pal who was staying with the Mortimers, an elderly English family who accommodate servicemen every week. Their bungalow stood in a large garden on the water edge. It had a tennis court, plenty of racquets, and a boat house and many boats, all at our disposal. Arum lilies were growing in profusion here, truly a dream place. A wooden pier ran from the boat house from the end of which you had a magnificent view of the valley.

Marjorie and Dawn took us over Mount Moab in the afternoon. We called at the quarry from which white stone

155

was being cut, most of which had been used at Canberra. We were shown round by Mr. Higgs. We clambered back over the hills and repaired to the Union. At night we stayed at the Canteen and helped cook the meal and entertain The Sisters, a jolly crowd of canteen volunteer workers. We met with a few Land Army girls and spent the night with them finally escorting them back to their billets across the golf links. As they were on duty we promised to call upon them the next night.

On Thursday we went to The Entrance and Tuggerah Lakes. The road to the Lakes was through a large orange grove and by Erina Creek and Avoca. The road cut through the bush and then we saw the Pacific Ocean riding high above the tree tops. The Entrance is delightful. There, white sandy beaches, heavy breakers, plenty of mullet, horse and hack riding and boating were there for your amusement. We walked over the bridge to Entrance North where a schoolmaster, Mr. Roberts, stopped us to have a conversation. He took us to meet his wife and have tea with them. There was plenty of conversation. They had two lads on Australian ships and a daughter at Sydney University. We motored back to Gosford, had tea, and went to the Land Army Hostel. Unfortunately it was late, and all except Billie and Gay Griffiths of one thousand and something Hunter Street, Newcastle, N.S.W. were in bed. It was a starry evening and we talked on the verandah. The scent of camellias filled the night air.

On Friday we lounged about, had a pub session in the late afternoon with Mr. Higgs and took him home to Hazeldawn where a party was thrown for us. Unfortunately Mr. Higgs went to sleep for three hours, well, it's hard work at the quarry. Among the guests were Mrs. Johnson, her daughter Mrs. Wetherall and her three children, and Ida Tonkins, a glamourous blonde who immediately set her cap at Alan, and invited us all to tea on Saturday. The evening was spent in playing the piano and pianola, singing, and dancing on the verandah. Mr. Higgs awoke and sang, he has a good voice. Mrs. Higgs not to let the side down gave a recitation of a stockrider who succumbed to foul drink and died a 'orrible death. I was not sure that Mrs. Higgs was ribbing us for our afternoon with Mr. Higgs. Still she's a great sport. On Saturday Mr. Higgs went to Sydney. Mrs. Higgs, this being her day off, but what she did during the week I do not know, took us to her favourite rendezvous, the Dogs. There was a line of bookies standing under coloured umbrellas feverishly chalking the odds of the races at Melbourne and Randwick, and accepting bets. Mrs. Higgs had a good day. I didn't back a winner. Of my choices one came in 2nd, two were 3rds, a 4th and a 5th I had, and the rest were well behind. I think my dogs had decided to sit down and enjoy the scenery.

We went to Ida's for tea, she had prepared a really good meal. Afterwards we met her friend, Ross, a nurse coming off duty at the station.

We left early on Sunday morning and caught the 07.20 for Sydney. The *Formidable* was in the Captain Cook Engraving Dock. We were told that we were going to Tokyo on the 19th to bring back prisoners of war. Conditions were none too good aboard, bathrooms flooded so it was going to the heads on the dockside. On Tuesday I met Doris Dodds and had dinner at Cahills then saw her home to Bardwell Park. I called at the Women's Weekly Club to see if Billie had registered there. The Club is tastefully appointed. I went for a sail round the bay in the afternoon.

On the 15th September I met Billie and had tea with her at the Club. Daphne and Sally joined us so we all went to Goat Island to dance. We caught the ferry at Circular Quay. The harbour lights were gleaming and illuminated the lawns on the island. The dance was a success. Afterwards, at their insistance, I took them to the King's Cross district, the flash but dubious area of Sydney. All the cafes were closed so Sally had to content herself by peering into the Arabian which looked seductive with its subdued lighting. On Saturday I called on Mary's people at Sailor Bay. We strolled around the district, climbed the knoll from which you have splendid views of the Middle Harbour. The show boats were gliding through the placid waters. The gardens were full of azaleas, nemetia, wisteria, lantana, certainly a blaze of colour. Mr. Wynn is a delightful gentleman, he was in opera for many years. Mrs. Wynn was in musical comedy. Afterwards there was a musical evening, songs and duets from Mary and her father, accompanied on the piano by Mrs Wynn. Violin solos from Mary. A very musical family. The rooms were furnished in good taste and there was a splendid library. One modern painting on the wall was of a gasometer, but then I am not a judge of modern art.

Tuesday, 18th September, and my birthday. First there was an inquiry into the loss of the Admiral's wine from a store next to mine. I received Commander's defaulters, but I will deal with that later. For my birthday. Billie took me to her uncle's house at Bronte. Bronte has a delightful bay with a splendid beach. Her uncle and aunt, Mr. and Mrs. Whittaker have a beautiful home called Clare. He is serving with the American Merchant Services. He emigrated from Salford in the twenties. The Whittakers have three daughters, Claire, Anne and Betty. Mr. and Mrs. Fish, who have a chain of butchers' shops, came round. We talked, played two-up, had supper and altogether had a most enjoyable evening especially in that they made the party my birthday party. Yes, they produced a wonderful birthday cake, the first I have ever had. All this had been planned without my knowledge. Hospitality plus.

We sailed on Wednesday the 19th September. The lower deck was cleared at 16.00 and the ship was dressed. It was a sunny afternoon, people on the domain waved farewell and soon we were passing Nielson Park, Sailor Bay, Watson's Bay and the Heads. That's Sydney, that was.

I now saw the Commander on a charge that I did negligently perform my duties. I was remanded to appear before the Skipper on the 21st.

158

This is what happened. On returning from leave at Gosford some radar equipment was required and radar ratings went to the store with me. To reach this store a hatch which is kept locked with a padlock has to be opened and permission to do so obtained. Below is a flat off which were two stores encased in strong mesh with doors which are also locked. One store was under my control and the other was in charge of the Captain's staff. On arrival at the hatch we found that it was already opened and stokers were pumping out flood water under the supervision of an Officer. My C.O. and W.O. nor any one else in our section were aware of this until I told them. As there were many civilians working on the ship and there were valuable instruments etc. in my store I asked the Engineering Officer in charge of the pumping party if he would put a guard on the hatch until it could be locked, or when the stokers were going for a meal or absent for other duties, so as to prevent unauthorised persons entering. This he agreed to do. I reported this to my C.O. and the W.O. and was complimented on my initiative. None of our section who were on duty when I was on leave also knew nothing about the flooding. I visited the store frequently to see what progress was being made, and checked my store to see that everything was in order. The other store was no concern of mine. The charge bewildered me. Items had been stolen from the Captain's store, not mine. Apparently Admiral Sir Philip Vian's wine had been placed in this store when he was on board and, on his leaving, it was found that £250 of wine was missing. The Skipper, naturally, was furious and decided that thieves had broken into his wine store, not bodily, but by removing bottles through a tiny hole in the dividing mesh between his store and mine. The hole was high up against the bulkhead, the wine had been stored yards away from the dividing mesh and the hole was so tiny that no bottle could possibly have passed through. Two Sub-Lieutenants who came down to inspect the stores failed to find the offending hole and when I pointed it out to them they stood there in total disbelief. I asked them

159

what size of bottle could possibly have been dragged through the mesh. They remained silent. The Admiral's Wine Steward's record showed that the wine had disappeared during my week's absence at Gosford. Any charge of negligence was, therefore, not mine but against any ratings on board at that time, if there were negligence, and more so against the persons in charge of the Captain's Store.

My defence at my trial was that I was not negligent because I was not on board at that time of the theft; that duty ratings on board at that time should be the ones to be questioned; that I had been praised on my initiative to protect the store when I returned. Unfortunately I gave the wrong name of the officer whom I approached, and could not change it. So to Lt. Boyd, an Australian Damage Control Officer, my sincerest apologies. The Skipper stifled all my arguments; at times there came from him frenetic screamings and banging on the deck with his fist; he would not allow me to call witnesses from the radar section who heard me ask for a guard to be put on the store and hatch. He demanded where I came from and when I answered; 'Manchester Sir,' he became hysterical and muttered, 'Northerners.' I would not be brow beaten and no doubt was answering with vehemence. I was stood down for punishment. The Master at Arms who lead me away advised me to be more respectful as he feared that I would get 98 days in cells. I was certain that all the Skipper wanted to do was to report to the Admiral that the culprit had been found and punished. I resumed duties and awaited the verdict, which I knew would not be a just one. I have never been in prison and wondered how I would respond to it, moreover my pride was hurt. And why should you not defend yourself?

I had to take some returns to the Paymaster Captain and he enquired how I had gone on and what was my sentence. I told him that I had been stood down for punishment, but I would refuse to do it, and I would appeal to the First Lord of the Admiralty, which was my right. He left me standing in his office. I had to appear again before the Skipper. Again another mock trial and screamings and desk bangings. Again I was stood down. Later my C.O. sent for me. He explained that the sentence which had originally been proposed had twice been reduced. I believe that he had defended me in private, but no officer defended me at the trials. I told my C.O. that I should not have been tried or charged at all, that enquiries should have been made from others. He sent for me again. He said that he had seen the Skipper personally and that if I would agree to a reduced sentence which would not affect my shore leave, as we would be at sea for many weeks; that my Good Conduct Badge would not be stripped from me in disgrace; that inconvenience would be minimal; that no adverse report or record would appear on my papers; could he go back to the Skipper and say that I would accept a lighter sentence.

I respected this officer, Lieutenant Commander Harry Barton, and the Paymaster Captain Claud Herdman, both Irishmen, and knew that they were doing their best to help me. I felt powerless and wondered whether the hassle was worth it. I understand the first proposed punishment had been reduced to 56 days cells, then 21 days cells and dip my badge. Now it was 14 days No. 11s, and 21 days stoppage of leave. I flatly refused to do the punishing drill otherwise I would accept although still protesting innocence. Somebody had to be punished, who it was did not matter.

As a consequence my routine for the next 14 days was to sling my hammock outside the Jaunty's office, and get a very early call to do chores before breakfast. You were allowed half an hour for dinner; muster at 17.00 and do two hours extra work or drill; muster again at 20.00 and 20.30 in No. 1s. There would be no make-and-mends if given, and on Sundays, such is the reverence for the day, you muster only at 20.30. You also did your usual work and watchkeeping duties. On Saturday, instead of the make-and-mend, the tannoy summoned the criminals of heinous crime to the Police Office. We lined up, all skates. A delightful chore had been chosen for us; paint the hangar

161

deck-head. 'Does anyone object?' demanded the Regulating Officer. One rating stepped forward. 'Any one else?' with a penetrating glance at me. I had had enough, and would my stepping forward constitute mutiny? I stood still, inwardly cursing myself. We were hoisted up by platform high up to the hangar deck head, separated, of course, there was to be no fraternising or skiving. The heat beat mercilessly down from the underside of the Flight Deck. There is little air to breathe up there. I commenced. I swallowed paint vapour, my eyes swam. Three hours later drenched in sweat and spotted in paint, I and the others were released. I had a shower and a hurried tea and did two more hours of punishing work. Other pleasing chores after being shaken were to scrub the galley deck clean of grease and spilled food. The kind C.P.O. did, however, reward our labours with a cup of char. And so to breakfast.

Sometime later I received a roundabout message that bottles of wine were being sold on the ship secretly. I approached my C.O. and asked permission to buy one if I were approached. He agreed. The suggestion was that this might be wine from the Captain's store and it was available because there had been collusion between someone with access to the Stores, and that the wine had not been stolen as suggested at my trial. I was not approached to buy a bottle. The days of jankers continued.

We arrived at the Admiralty Isles on the 25th September and at Leyte on the 28th. The following days we passed islands covered with dark green forests on our way to Manila. Here all we could see through the mist when we arrived on the 30th was the shadows of tall buildings. Rain was falling in torrents. We were to take on board, but because of the dangerously rough seas, the I.L.C.'s were lying to and not discharging prisoners of war for repatriation. Signals were made to the I.L.C.'s telling them to drop anchor and we would draw alongside them, but no prisoners of war embarked and food prepared for them was wasted. The prisoners of war finally came on board on the

162

5th October. The sea had been calm all day but by tea time when the first batch arrived it was cutting up rough again. Skipper was screaming to Guns on the camel to take in the head slack and the prisoners took up the chorus. The gangway was in danger of being crushed in between the camel and I.L.C. The sea between was squeezed into a geyser and she and the camel ebbed and flowed. Camp beds and kit bags were being flung across the constantly widening gulf and many men tried to jump. Ratings helped the Australians over and finally the plank was secured after many had crossed by jumping. They filed into the forward lift well and received chocolate, cigarettes, periodicals, sleeping and ship information. Hands relieved them of their kit bags and led them to their quarters, the arrangements worked smoothly. The hangar had been cleared of all aircraft and was now a hospital ward. Soon the newcomers were appearing on deck, munching buns, talking to us, or wandering along and looking in wonder at everything. Deck chairs had been placed on the flight deck and these were soon occupied. Many buried themselves in the newspapers. The ice was soon broken. They were talking. They wore American clothing, green/khaki trousers, shirts, underpants, big clumsy boots and Digger hats. Some had souvenirs, Jap swords and money. The ship had a holiday appearance, deck chairs and newspapers. We weighed anchor at 19.00. The *Colossus* hallooed us. A hospital ship passed by us. Side lights flung their flare on the deck and we said Goodbye to Manila. We passed many islands all day—dark and light green masses against a calm blue sea. We listened to their stories—harrowing stories of five years of captivity in the hands of a sadistic regime, and some of the officers did not come out of it unscathed. On Sunday one of the re-patriots died and was buried at sea. We attended the service on the Q.D. He was buried at 16.30. The Union Jack barely fluttered, the air was so still. Marine guards fired, the last post sounded. The C-of-E chaplain conducted the service which was attended by the R.C. padre.

We arrived at Sydney on the 14th October to tumultous cheers from headlands, ferries, quays, and everywhere. The prisoners had a rousing reception from relatives and friends and had a ticker tape reception in Sydney.

On the 18th I went to Corrimal renewing acquaintance with the Sutherlands. The stay was short and well worth while. On Sunday, 21st I went to Bronte with a view of calling on the Whittakers and finding out whether Billie had managed to get any leave. Her home was in Newcastle, a very high number in a very long road, and I had lost her address. Unfortunately no one was in. The beach was crowded. Brightly coloured bathing costumes enlivened the straw coloured beach. It looked like one of those paintings where the colours are highly exaggerated. We walked along the beach which is much bigger than Blackpool but prettier. I had tea with Mary on the 22nd and afterwards saw The Desert Song.

On the 23rd October my life aboard the *Formidable* was terminated. I am now going to interrupt the narrative and link the past with the present. Months ago I was climbing the ladder to the Captain's Request Desk, spotless in my tropical rig, when Jimmy the One was descending. I stepped on one side to let him pass when he stopped me. He was his usual all seeing self. He asked if I were applying for my Leading Rate (only 3 years too late, for I had qualified for it and for certain reasons had not applied). I told him I was applying for my badge of 3 years of undetected crime, officially Good Conduct Badge, and he replied he would be seeing my C.O. about me. My C.O. sent for me the following morning, he had my papers on his desk. He asked why I had not applied for promotion and what had happened at the interview into the recommendation made in London that I should be considered for a commission. I gave him my opinion of the interview. He instructed me to apply forthwith for my Leading Rate, then after a month for P.O. rate, which would undoubtedly be automatic. Then I could study and sit for C.P.O. I refused. Now my release

164

had come and I was asked to stay on board. It was hoped the ship would be returning to the U.K. and little or no difference in time of arriving there would arise. My knowledge of the radar etc., stores would facilitate de-storing. I was not to mention the impending departure to the U.K. I remembered that we had been on our way to Vancouver and were within 24 hours of docking there when we were re-routed. I had had an idea that if I were put ashore at Vancouver I would try and reach Medicine Hat where distant relatives of friends had emigrated years ago. I preferred, therefore, to take my chance of going to the transit camp at Sydney for transfer to the U.K.

Before I left the ship I had a most pleasant surprise. I was waiting with my kit-bag and hammock on a weather deck waiting for the boat to take me to the *Golden Hind* at Warwick Farm. I was definitely merry with the sippers, a custom of tasting everyone's rum on special occasions, but capable of walking even if speech might be a little incoherent, when the Paymaster Captain and the Paymaster Commander appeared on the weather deck. Both had come to wish me good luck on my return to civvy street and shook my hand, such was their efficiency and caring attitude. I was hoping they would not smell the rum in my throat, and I thought I was in for another spot of jankers. Just my luck, I was thinking, but I escaped. I still have a wonderful regard for the *Formidable*.

We left by lorry (the boat) and trailer and en route nearly came to grief. The trailer arm snapped but despite staggering, we were brought to a standstill and finally got a new lorry.

H.M.S. *Golden Hind* is situated next to the Racecourse at Warwick Farm, about an hour's run outside Sydney. It is a huge camp of pre-fabricated buildings situated in lovely pastoral scenery. We found the food was excellent and the sleeping accommodation in the huts roomy. A good canteen provided snacks, ice cream, coca-cola, beer if you queued long enough. It was loafers' paradise here. Thousands strolled around doing nothing. You could take days in doing joining routine, if you were so inclined. The place seemed over-staffed and there were many ratings who had high A.S.G. and no sea time. Some barrack stanchions had never been to sea except in the ship which brought them out. I did practically no work the time I was there and up to the time I left the entries in the records of the Stores Staff would have been completed in 10 minutes aboard the *Formidable*. They got shore leave at 15.45 one night and 16.00 the next, with an afternoon off during the week and make-and-mends on Saturdays and Sundays. Compared with life aboard, Action Stations, long hours, this was a life of luxury and idleness. There were some drawbacks, no mirrors in the wash places, no tables to write at, or chairs to sit down, at least where we were accommodated, and sand everywhere.

Edgar Hartley whom I came on draft with, got posted to the *Quality* on the 27th. I am hoping to go on the *Devonshire* early next week. Edgar waited in the baggage store from 10.15 until 15.30 before transport arrived. I helped him stack his luggage on the lorry and waved him farewell. Two hours later he was back, the *Quality* was not in Sydney but was at Melbourne. Anyhow he left two days later by destroyer to the *Quality*.

The Parade Ground of the *Golden Hind* was the mustering point each day of ratings awaiting draft to the U.K. We gathered untidily and were constantly admonished to 'get fell in in sixes'. Apparently there were no mathematicians among us, or was 6 an unlucky number which we must not observe. We milled around especially as the voice of the R.P.O. barely carried beyond a few yards. You stood for hours waiting.

After a few days of this circus I thought that I would practise what a Writer on the *Formidable* had told me how to get on the list. I disbelieved him at the time. I entered the Drafting Office through a door marked 'PRIVATE. NO ADMITTANCE', into a huge hall with writers at separate desks. I enquired of the possibility of my name being called

166

out for passage to the U.K. in the next few days, and mimed payment of a back-hander. This reminded me of the time when I was awaiting call-up to the R.N. and was impatient to go. I phoned the office dealing with the call-up to enquire how long it would be for my turn to go. I heard what I thought to be index cards being flicked over, and then I was told that I was well down the list. I asked if my name could be pushed forward. He expressed disbelief at what I had asked but I persuaded him that I wanted to go as soon as possible. I was called up within a few days. Now the reverse was happening. On the following Monday morning I waited from 10.15 to 12.15 when my name was called out for the *Devonshire* draft. I did not go back and give the back-hander. If the practice is true then they must be taught a lesson. It might be a coincidence, however.

I went ashore that night to do some shopping. I met Bungy Williams so we went to Cahills for tea. Perhaps I had better describe what I had as it will be a long time before I have another like it. I had a salad consisting of lettuce hearts, paw-paw, pineapple, radish, celery, cream cheese, chopped parsley, and mayonnaise. I finished with a lemon meringue base in the form of a shell filled with lemon paste, and topped with cream and nuts, followed by coffee. I wrote a few farewell letters to my Australian friends and returned to the *Golden Hind*. We left here on Tuesday the 30th at 3.15 p.m. by special train to Sydney.

A hitch occurred during the morning as the *Devonshire* could not accommodate all the draft and so 150 deletions had to be made. These were transferred to a troopship, the *Andes*, leaving on the 3rd November. Buses awaited us at Central Station and we were taken down to Wooloomooloo. Our names were hailed from the midships and we ascended a wobbly gangway. I was assigned to Mess 32. Thirteen of us occupied this mess which was originally FXL Ord. Seamen. The messes were overcrowded, but who cared and, after *Formidable*, were not so clean. The bathrooms were primitive, a few enamel bowls hung over a trough. No showers and one tap per bathroom. Food was good. We slipped at 15.15 on Wednesday, 31st October.

Our mess was very mixed: R.A.F., Fleet Air Arm, Canteen Assistants, Writers and Supply. No Messman. Jock McCall, of Costorphine, and late of *Formidable*, the irrepressible one, came on board at one of our calling places but I was ashore. I believe he had everyone rolling on the deck.

I was assigned to Naval Stores and found that the work was less than negligible. One complete loaf. It was choppy going through the Heads when leaving Sydney but afterwards the *Devonshire* behaved. Not so in the Australian Bight. Here was a dancing horizon and a floundering sea. Everyone was happy to sling hammocks and turn in. The fugginess between decks did not help. A cloud of moths passed over the ship one day blanketing the sky. Many porpoises and dolphins were seen. We reached Fremantle on the 5th November. I managed a shopping run to Perth. The bus route was through scrubby sandy land and bathing beaches. Perth is a lovely city on the Swan River with plenty of fine shops and handsome buildings. The streets are broad and clean and a good sized park added to the spaciousness of the place. I slept at the Sportsmen's Club in Fremantle that night and returned on board in glorious sunshine at 07.30.

We sailed to Colombo on the 6th leaving at 08.00. Whales were spouting and a school of flying fish ribbed the sea in their effort to avoid us. Many sooty tern were seen. We passed the Cocos Isles, the scene of the sinking of the German raider, *Embden*, in the last war, by H.M.A.S. *Sydney*.

The weather was now much hotter and awnings were spread. We worked tropical routine, that is mornings only, and slept in the afternoons under the awnings or wherever there was shade. Gramophone recitals were given on the 4" Gun Platform. Many birds were seen, sooty tern and wideawakes, short tail sheerwaters, and the booby bird which is not unlike the English gannet. On the 11th

November we crossed the equator and held an Armistice Service on the Q.D. The hymns sung were: 'Through all the changing scenes of life', and 'O God of Bethel'. The sky and the sea were a faultless blue, the awning a spotless cream, and the gun cover a suffused gold. Colombo was reached on the 12th and I went ashore. I made a few purchases; a necklace of moonstones, the lucky stones of Ceylon; and some satinwood book ends. I saw the wood carvers at work in their dirty tumble down shop where rain leaked through the roof. They carve with broken knives and chisels the most exquisite pieces of art from king ebony, rosewood, satinwood. Mere children were sitting cross legged on the earthen floor holding and carving wood between their feet. It was raining that night as I walked through the stinking streets of Slave Island which were alive with muffled voices, whilst ghostly figures glided by silently in their long white robes.

On the 13th I went ashore on duty to Kochakadde. I passed through Slave Island and by the red and yellow stone Buddhist Temple surrounded by dirty hovels of homes. The streets were filled with native traders: the earthenware dealer, tinsmith, baker, sellers of coffee, meal and old junk. Women in brightly coloured dresses went about in groups; old beggars crippled and deformed chanted high pitched demands for alms; youngsters in long gowns noisily dodged in and out of the crowds. The market sent up a piercing stink to heaven.

I could not buy an ounce of tea. There was a sales quota and I did not come at the right time.

We sailed at 18.00 on the 13th and on the 14th passed the Minicoy Islands. These are the usual coconut palm islands. They were crescent shaped and have a leper colony; the nearby island is a smallpox colony. Now we're running into the trade winds which herald the monsoon. We passed the *Northeray* on which a mutiny took place on the 6th October. The culprits were sentenced to five years and four years servitude. One wonders how decent lads are driven to this extent, could it be the conditions under which we serve? On the 17th we saw the north east coast of Africa and on the 20th arrived at Port Tewfik. Swarms of locusts had been flying over the ship and a few pelicans had been seen.

I landed at Port Tewfik and took a taxi to Suez. Here was the usual town of shops, high smells and dimly lit streets. Touts all around were persuading you to buy coshes, knives and other curios. Some brightly coloured belligerents, the Italians, were much in evidence. I bought an ivory gazelle. We walked by the railway line, which runs alongside the main street, off which was a side street entirely draped with carpets from wall to wall and on the street level where a Mohammedan service was taking place. We walked back to the causeway to Port Tewfik which is much cleaner than Suez. There were tree lined streets, an open air cinema and a graceful church on the quayside.

We reached Port Said on the 21st November and I did see this time the statue of de Lessops on the water front. On the way through Suez were many tall masted flat bottomed boats, endless sand dunes and water covered flats.

I re-visited Alexandria going to the Native Bazaars to shop. A young native boy called Morgan cottoned on to me and, although I could have 'imshied' him I was amused by his constant regard that I purchased what I wanted and at the right price. Admittedly he shepherded me to his pals for my purchases and bargained heatedly over prices and warned against imitations and high prices. It was an amazing show he put on and I really enjoyed it. I would refuse to buy goods which I thought too dear despite tremendous reductions in price.

One of my new messmates wanted a suitcase and, as he could not get ashore he asked me to buy one for him. We tried one or two shops and were not satisfied so Morgan took me to where they were manufactured. It was down a back street, down which I would not have ventured alone, the workshop was a hovel in a backyard. I examined the leather cases being made and explained what I wanted. They would make me one while I waited. A chair was

170

brought for me and a cup of coffee as I watched the work being done. The linings they had for the inside were not to my satisfaction, quite garish colours, so they sent for other material for my inspection and choosing. Morgan, I asked him was he a relative of Captain Morgan, but he did not understand, chatted away with his warnings and kept me amused whilst my purchase was made. I don't know who gave him this name, but this good looking youngster, with the gravity and acumen of a grown up, and yet with a constantly smiling face enhanced with gleaming teeth, enlivened my four hours of shopping. On a purchase being completed, 'What did I want next? Yes I know the very place where you can get it cheap and not imitation.' So it went on. We dodged in and out of shops, saw goods and bargained, first me then Morgan. Out we would go, the goods unbought, and Morgan agreeing, 'Too dear, I know another place cheaper and not imitation.' It was excellent fun and I did not mind having my leg pulled. I wanted a pair of sandals for myself. Through bazaars and crowded streets we rushed, Morgan carrying the suitcase with distinct pride and flourish. We stopped at a street trader's handcart piled high with sandals. I tried a pair on—a chair was produced from nowhere in that crowd of onlookers. The street vendor was probably more than forty years of age, and wanted 60 ackers. I bargained him down to 40 but, as he put them in the case Morgan tugged my sleeve and told me the vendor was motherless. I was so overcome by remorse I gave him the extra 20. Morgan smiled, was it a benediction? 'Silk?' 'Too dear,' said Morgan, 'and not worth it. It's 120 a metre.' This lad is an expert on everything. I had very little money left, and Morgan knew it, but to prove his statement he took me to a silk store and had all the rolls of silk laid out for my appreciation and then calmly told the shopkeeper that we were not buying. It was now time for me to get a snack with the little money I had yet Morgan insisted on showing me the way to Mohammet Ali Square. I gave him a few shillings for his entertainment, help and amusing company. He was so delighted that he insisted that I visit his father who was selling fruit from a barrow and gave me a bunch of bananas into the bargain. God bless you Morgan, or Allah, you certainly deserve it.

We left Alexandria on the 23rd November. I won't say much about the Mediterranean, I've said it all before. I'll just say we passed Malta and Sicily, and Pantallaria, and called at Gibraltar on the 27th November. On the 28th we passed Lisbon and on the 30th we arrived at Devonport, Guz, in glorious sunshine. I left Devonport by bus for the station, passing Pennycomequick, and entrained for Portsmouth, arriving at 2 am on the 1st December.

We unloaded our gear from the trucks then hung about in M Block where we had a cup of tea, after which we breakfasted. The occupants of the hammocks had an uncomfortable night with the constant passing and repassing of 200 ratings in and out of their quarters. We received 14 days leave that afternoon.

I returned to Pompey on the 17th December for demobilisation. From here I went to Stamshaw where all particulars were taken and a medical examination was given.

Later we were kitted up with civilian clothes in a converted garage. The system was excellent and the staff were most helpful. I chose a brown coloured suit which fitted, a pair of shoes, one shirt and two collars, a tie, a trilby hat, a raincoat, and a pair of studs. That was on the 19th December, 1945. A bus took us from the garage, now a clothing store, to the station.

At last I was free. I shall always remember the comradeship and the loyalty of those who serve in the Royal Navy. If I had to go again I hope that the Navy would accept me. It was my home.